The Psychology of Self~ Destr

GOING MAD
TO STAY SANE

ANDY WHITE

Typeset by Jonathan Downes, Corinna Downes
Cover and Layout by SPiderKaT for CFZ Communications
Using Microsoft Word 2000, Microsoft , Publisher 2000, Adobe Photoshop CS.

First published in Great Britain by CFZ Press

CFZ Press
Myrtle Cottage
Woolsery
Bideford
North Devon
EX39 5QR

© CFZ MMXV

ISBN: 978-1-909488-32-8

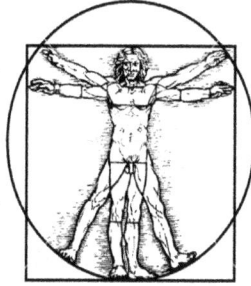

Preface

Addictions, neuroses, depressions and despairs are self-destructive behaviours. We howl 'why did this happen to me? Or 'why did this happen to me - again?' This book explores a myth which helps us understand envious self-attack, suggesting there is always meaning hidden in such acts. In the Greek myth, King Midas is granted a wish by Dionysus, a Trickster God. He can literally turn things into gold. Unfortunately, food, drink and even his beautiful daughter become real gold. Midas has 'golden objects', but he can't use them. A starting point for most neuroses is not getting what we existentially need: inner security which comes from being allowed to be who we truly are. This often arises from deep experiences of insecurity during childhood. With an insecure inner world, our outer world falls apart. We destroy it, greedy for success, attention, gold and power. We become consumers of natural resources and each other rather than creative producers.

Midas's greed is understood here as his struggle to fill an empty space. This is like 'part-object relating' instead of 'whole object' relating - 'you are only useful to me because you can do X for me.' rather than 'we value each other simply because we exist.' Full of remorse, Midas seeks out the Trickster God. Dionysus tells him to find a sacred spring, drink, be cleansed and become ordinary again. It is humbling for the King to admit he made a terrible mistake.

His story needs a context - a family setting. We meet Cybele, Midas's terrible witch mother, who castrated his brother Attis to keep him as her faithful priest. In self-destructive behaviour we might orbit a 'terrible mother goddess', (a persecuting internal object) making ourselves impotent to try to win her love. Midas's father Gordius, a typical 'absent father', set his son an impossible task - undo the Gordian knot and win the Kingdom. Alexander the Great beat Midas to it: he simply cut the knot in half with his sword.

Midas tragedy stemmed from a troubled family: seeking to meet impossible parental demands, he made an impossible request. He didn't see his request was Non-Sense. Turning things gold - object relating into thing making - turned his world to lead, a negative alchemy. Self-destructive behaviour arises from trying to please an unpleasable parent, trying to be a 'golden child' instead of a real one. If we can't make or use secure internal parental objects then we can't make symbolic, inner gold from negative experiences so we have to make material, outer gold from everything and everyone else. Power takes the place of love. We become 'an evil Doctor in a secret underground volcano lair planning to take over the world'.

Any pattern of self destructiveness, whether it is drug or alcohol misuse, eating disorder, compulsive sexuality, creating financial or criminal disasters, tends to repeat - better the devil we know. Midas cut himself off from intimacy, becoming isolated, alienated and maddened. He used 'either-or' thinking: 'either it's gold, or it is worthless' - reducing his world to a competition about value rather than a co-operation in valuing. Jung repeatedly said 'Self is a collective': Self is a collective noun, referring to a large group of possibilities. If we are to find gold in suffering, we can only do this by sharing in the suffering of others and allowing others to see and share our own. In tragedies of self-destruction, on a personal and on a global level, we need to find how to curb the greedy violence we direct at ourselves and our planet. We can't do so till we acknowledge common ownership and a shared stewardship . . . that Self is a collective. .

Midas was a fool who persisted in his folly and became wise. Greed deprived him of access to life in a way he could not ignore. We may not remember analytic theories, or find developmental or archetypal metaphors speak to our condition. When we are 'going off on one' it can be warm and comforting - 'I've been wronged! I demand . . .' sadly, this makes thinking impossible because there's nothing to think about: we are entitled - aren't we? Reflecting on this myth shows a way out of self-destruction comes when we recognise what we're doing, wash off pathological entitlement and admit our Self is bigger than our Ego: that is, the psychological function we call Self seeks coherence, continuity, agency and affective relating and operates at a deeper level than our ego-function, which is concerned with moment-to-moment reality testing.

Stories, especially myths, particularly when well interpreted, always speak to our condition. They talk in symbols, which turn words into gold. I find myself reflecting on two examples from this text: 'Nonsense is the language of the soul in exile', and 'The only way out of neurotic pain is to experience the real pain that lies beneath it'. I can hold onto these ideas when I'm feeling self destructive. I can use this beautifully retold myth when I'm with patients, or myself. It is easy to remember to wonder 'am I having a Midas moment here? Am I being greedy for attention, greedy to "get it right" - or am I washing in a still pool?'

Analysts and therapists receive 'magical transferences' - people imagine we can turn their lead into gold *for* them, rather than show them how to do this for themselves. Midas reminds me not to become inflated or grandiose, imagining I can or ought meet such requests. This text gives a simple and passionate twist to an old story, which helps make new and better stories about our worst mistakes. It gives me, as a reader, a sense of hope when I see how I create my own despair.

Analysis is about making the complex simple. This book shows us a myth about a man who made the simple, complex. Neurotic moments are our Self trying to talk to us when we won't, don't or can't listen. Whether it is a small act of sabotage (going out and forgetting our keys), or a big one (repeatedly forming compulsive and destructive relationships), when we are 'beside ourselves' with frustration, Andy White suggests, we have a moment when our Self is trying to be beside us. If we learnt to ask 'what does this mean?' we could stop repeating a pattern.

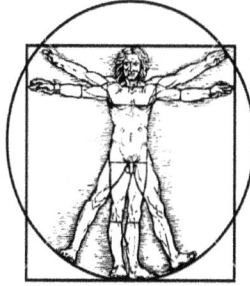

Introduction

I f a fool persists in his folly', says William Blake, 'he will become wise.' This is a rule. We tend to think of life's folly as superfluous to requirements. We feel burdened, limited, even cursed by the irrational problems that place such restrictions on the way we'd like to live our lives. We spend much of the time feeling the effects of our folly, trying to 'work out' our problems, or figuring ways to be rid of the psychological demons that plague us.

We rarely stop to think what the need for neurosis might be, or what purpose these quirks of the psyche might serve. The resolution to our self-destructiveness would seem to be in head-on conflict. The smoker uses brute force to quit. The anorexic makes herself eat, or is made to. The depressive coerces himself out of bed. All manner of cognitive and/or behavioural techniques are brought to bear on the now doubly unfortunate.

It fails to occur to us that the tenacity of our neuroses is for reasons far greater than their seeming need to create misery in our lives, that the symptoms of our dis-ease are precisely the statement of the soul's discomfort which, because we will not heed its knocking at our door, must come in by the window.

The pain, the despair, the craziness of self-destructiveness is as loud a statement as it is possible to make that the soul is in exile and under attack. Very often our problem is not so much that we suffer from self-destructiveness, but that we hold it at arm's length and in so doing deprive ourselves of its instruction. The source of our suffering is as much our ivory towered existence and antagonism to realities deeper than those of our narrow self-image, as it is the blows of fate from which we are so keen to defend ourselves. If we cannot or will not hear the soul's rumblings, then it will find some artful way of rubbing our noses in that to which we needs must pay attention.

The purpose of this book is to try to get to the bottom of the phenomenon of self-destructiveness, to account for it in some way, to understand the soul's purpose in visiting violence upon itself. I am going to use the myth of Midas to create a context for this exploration.

The story of Midas - that he was granted a wish to turn things into gold - is well known, but the full story contains all kinds of subtleties that indicate both how he got himself into such a mess and also how he may get himself out of it. Despite its origins in antiquity the myth of Midas has a timeless quality to it, one that permits us to draw its wisdom into a contemporary context and hopefully to find the possibility of a resolution to one of the most pressing problems of our age. Perhaps now more than ever, we are obliged to pay attention to the tragedies of self-destruction, both on a personal and on a global level, to find some way of curbing the violence we perpetrate against ourselves and our planet.

Midas was a fool who persisted in his folly and became wise. To begin with, however; he was no more than an unreflective simpleton who was unable or unwilling to consider the consequences of his wish. In so far as this is true, Midas represents the neurotic principle of self-destructiveness in us all. He could have asked Dionysus, the dark god who granted him this wish, for wisdom or peace or contentment, but this would have entailed the acknowledgement that he was not wise or that he was consumed with inner strife or smitten by discontent. Such admissions would have offended his self-image and entailed a descent into the personal chaos of such an intimate confession. For the want of this truth-telling he is forced to invite a self-destructive neurosis upon himself in the form of a wish for something that ultimately chokes him.

It's all very attractive to begin with, and Midas delights in turning first one thing then another into gold. This is the way with neurosis. Substance abuse, compulsive sexuality, obsessive dieting or the grandiose hauteur of a superiority complex are all fun to begin with. They both mask the underlying emptiness and produce a temporary feeling of well being. So Midas is content for a while. Then he gets hungry and calls for food, but as soon as he picks up the dainty titbits they turn to gold. The neurosis is pretty but it cannot feed or nurture.

Midas feels disconcerted but contents himself with turning some more things into gold, almost as though he needs to confirm the wisdom of his decision. Then he sees his daughter. She runs to him and he embraces her, remembering too late the consequences, and she too becomes a cold ornament to add to his growing collection of comfortless things. This might well be the point at which Midas would like to 'get rid' of his neurosis and indeed he begs Dionysus to revoke the golden touch, but the dark god refuses and makes him go deeper into the experience, sensing perhaps some opportunity in Midas' foolish wish.

Midas begins to realise that the granting of his wish is making explicit something that had been going on for some time. His meaning lies outside himself. He has a habit of depersonalising others, a way of turning people into objects. Having found emptiness and isolation in what he imagined would fulfil him, Midas is forced to reassess his values and face the deeper reality which the neurosis was intended to conceal but has ultimately brought into the light of day. This is ever the situation with the unconscious. If we will not face our shadow then it must be revealed through some other means. Sooner or later the neurosis will lead us directly to that which it intended to hide and lay bare whatever it is we actually require in order to be made whole, despite our aversion.

If we get rid of the neurosis by treating it behaviourally or by reducing the symptoms with drugs then the lesson it has to teach us can never be learnt. If Dionysus simply revoked the wish then Midas would be none the wiser; but Dionysus is smart. He lets Midas sit with his symptoms long enough to realise the inner experience that the self-destructive wish was unconsciously designed to obscure. This has the effect of balancing Midas' arrogance and pride. It makes him more human, more approachable, more aware of his ordinariness and his vulnerabilities. He takes the time to bemoan his folly, to drink his bitter cup to the full, to see the error of his former pride, the shallowness of his former values, the absence of meaning and the loss of purpose.

Eventually Dionysus relents, but not by simply recanting the wish. He could have done but chose not to. Instead he tells Midas that if he wishes to be truly free he must go and wash himself in the source of the river Pactolus some distance away. Dionysus is crafty, and in fact a god of considerable compassion. He knows full well that this task will deepen Midas' experience of himself, and return him to a more authentic way of living.

Ultimately our self-destruction will point the way to our salvation. This is the poetry and the paradox of the psyche. The symptom that leads one away from soul is also the signpost that returns us. Midas follows the signpost through to the very end, first out of wanton lust and avoidance, then out of desperation and finally in humble complicity as he makes the penitent's pilgrimage to the fountainhead of the river, itself a symbol of soul. He rejuvenates himself in its life-giving waters having endured a solitary journey.

On this journey he is caught between the chaos of his neurotic existence and the chaos of a radical shift in identity, a time of betwixt and between, a threshold of initiation where the neurosis is transformed into the deeper experience it represented but could never quite embody. What the ego decides for the soul has become what the soul chooses for itself with the ego's consent.

In the process the ego is transmuted and Midas becomes a new man. The outer gold of the neurosis is realised as the inner gold of transfiguration and Midas emerges from the waters refreshed and complete. Midas could never have got here directly. He had to go via his neurosis, letting its experience inform him of the soul's needs. With the help of Dionysus' compassionate understanding that the neurotic wish held the germ of a more profoundly symbolic request, the neurosis was not lifted but lived through, as all life with its pains and woes must be lived through. The neurotic short cut shows us what is wanted, but not how to get there or how to understand its message.

For as long as we are focused on this outer gold-making we will suffer from what we could call the Midas syndrome. This is a state of psychological dis-ease characterised by self-destructiveness, a sense of isolation, insatiable dissatisfaction and rampant image-making that knows no bounds. What we need to ask in the face of a syndrome of such epidemic proportions is how things have come to such a pass, and how we may free ourselves from its possession. We might find some answers by starting with Midas' own family and looking at some of the circumstances of his childhood. What we will discover is a blueprint for the family set-up that produces self-destructiveness. Self-destructive behaviour always has a context. If we are to understand self-destructiveness we need to begin with the milieu into which the self-destructive character is born.

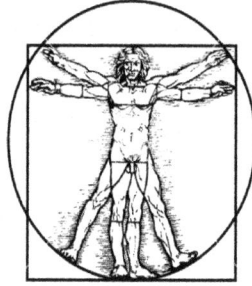

1
Cybele - the Devouring Mother

The negative form of the Great Mother can bring life to a halt, evoke emotional emptiness, petrification, blockage of the creative imagination and of ... potency.

M. Jacoby

Midas' mother was Cybele, a dark and dangerous goddess who dwelt in mountain caves and had as her following a retinue of self-castrated priests. This tradition began with Cybele's vengeful emasculation of her son Attis, half brother to Midas, who dared find himself a lover of his own choosing. Not only did Cybele deprive him of this choice, but she also sent him into an insane frenzy during which he castrated and killed himself. Cybele then resurrected Attis in order to occupy the post of consort for which she had always intended him. Here, in a nutshell, is the devouring mother diverting her offspring for her own purposes and the self-destruction that invariably follows.

It's important for us to recognise at the outset that the story of Midas is not just a metaphor for masculine psychology. For our purposes both Midas and Attis can be construed as androgynous figures, and their trials at the hands of Cybele as pertaining to both sexes. Cybele's castration of Attis is a symbol of disempowerment that the negative mother can wreak on both her male and female offspring alike. It's a statement that says 'you will not be potent, live your own life or become your own person. You belong to me.' Likewise the figure of Cybele, though represented in female form is equally alive and active in fathers who invade their progeny for their own purposes, who use their children as extensions of their own egos and buttresses for their secretly insecure sense of self.

Psychology books on developmental theory tell us *ad nauseam* how the child experiences itself to one degree or another in a state of union with the mother, only gradually separating itself and becoming autonomous. What is little mentioned, and perhaps out of embarrassment, is that this symbiosis is also true for the parent. Adults who have had their innocence stripped from them, or who are at least in mortal combat with fate to prevent this from happening, who are furthermore becoming increasingly aware of their lost youth, their missed opportunities, failed dreams and to cap it all - impending death, cannot help but live their lives vicariously through their offspring in order to avoid these looming and unpleasant realities.

Children must covertly collude with all this and allow themselves to be undermined in order to preserve the *status quo* and keep the pathway to mother clear. Cybele experiences her aliveness vicariously through the child and so the child must harness itself to her needs. She is subject to what R.D. Laing calls 'ontological dependency' which means that her experience of being, of existing, is bound up in her offspring. The experience of relationship based on genuine mutuality is substituted for this dependence upon which her very being has become conditional.

Utter detachment and isolation (withdrawal to her mountain cave) are regarded as the only alternative to a claim of vampire-like attachment in which the other person's life blood is necessary for one's own survival.

This course of action will backfire on Cybele. When she affords either of her offspring the power to give her life meaning she must inadvertently become even further depersonalised in the process since this kind of dependence is an admission, albeit covert, that she is unable to find meaning within her own subjective reality. She might defend herself from this unpleasantness momentarily by depersonalising them in turn, as indeed she does when she sends Attis mad, resurrecting him as a modified thing to be used for her convenience, but even this must ultimately fail to protect her from her secret fears. 'The more one attempts to preserve one's autonomy and identity by nullifying the specific human individuality of the other, the more it is felt to be necessary to do so, because with each denial of the other person's ontological status, one's own security is decreased, the threat to the self from the other is potentiated and hence has to be even more desperately negated.' (Laing, 1960).

Whichever way Cybele chooses to use the child as a crutch for her insecurity, either by depersonalising and withdrawing from him or by invading him and urging him to identify with her, all these efforts must fail. If she depersonalises the child with her cold withdrawal she further aggravates her own feelings of unreality. If, on the other hand, she uses the child to bolster the buckling bulwarks of her insecurity she must by implication acknowledge his value and in fact his power over her, power that can, in the end, only fuel the experience of her own impotence.

Cybele oscillates interminably between the engulfment and abandonment of her offspring, trying in vain to find some way of using the child as a shield from the terror of her own insubstantiality and laying her failure to accomplish this firmly at the child's door. The child accepts the responsibility - not because it can do anything about the Mother's predicament but because its own being is at stake and because some contact, even accusation and blaming, is better than nothing at all.

Cybele needs her offspring to tend her and revolve around her despite their inability to do anything really effective. Though nothing can come of it the roles of caring are reversed. The child's need to be at the centre of things is experienced as an act of usurpation by Cybele. The child soon learns that to be at the centre, to succeed, to be focused upon, is equivalent to an act of theft, theft that is punishable by abandonment, withdrawal and a pervasive feeling of guilt.

Alan is an artist. For many years he has produced nothing of consequence. Then one day a piece that he has made is invited on tour with a show funded by a local council. He's pleased but unaccountably panicky about it. He tells no one of his success, and realises he's spent his life keeping such secrets. He's afraid of the limelight. What is it that is so frightening about the limelight? 'It means that the limelight is taken away from others', he says. His limelight, his success, is perceived as stealing from 'the others', and for much of his life this was so. Mother was the centre of attention and for him to take attention for himself was to take it away from her, risking her cold wrath and silent enmity.

Alan becomes depressed as a compromise solution, pushing down the inspiration, the life force, that threatens to detract from her limelight. He limps through life and, Christlike, dies inside so that 'others' might live. This is the perennial story of Cybele's child who must bleed itself dry and deaden itself so that Mother can feel alive, must depersonalise itself so that Mother can feel like a person, must live in limbo so that the source of its life might feel sufficiently contained to spare her offspring a thought.

Cybele plants herself in the centre of family life in an unconscious attempt to make up for the violence and lack of attention she herself received as a child. She becomes manipulative and controlling in this unacknowledged urgency to get her needs met. If the child fails to respond to this moody prima donna, as indeed it must, then she either flounces off to her mountain cave giving her child the silent treatment until it mends its ways and makes a visible conciliatory show of playing the game by her rules, or she flies into a hysterical tantrum and collapses. 'She would go cold on me', says a young man of his Cybelian mother. 'It would go on for days at a time. If I stepped out of line it was like a personal offence, as though I'd deliberately slighted her by taking attention onto myself. So I'd rush around doing little things to show I was sorry, little gestures to demonstrate that I was thinking about her, that I'd stopped making demands of her and was willing to make her the focus of my life again. Then the thaw would melt and it was suddenly like the days of iciness had never been. We were one again.'

The Cybelian parent is often 'very close' to her offspring. To the world, and sometimes even to the child, she appears to be the very embodiment of the good mother. But her 'closeness' has an insidious quality. She's too close, she's 'over-protective'. Their closeness is not the closeness of contact where relationships can be experienced. Their closeness is the closeness of the pressgang. It is the 'closeness' of unconscious identification.

The experience of difference which is essential to authentic relationship cannot be tolerated. Separateness is experienced as an attack. Accusations of betrayal lurk in the child's every autonomous act. This closeness is invariably dressed up as a virtue by the child, 'we're really similar', ' … we're more like sisters', '… she can tell me anything, really treats me like an adult', ' … she trusts me with her innermost secrets'. The undercurrent of abandonment is lost in the glow of 'specialness' that identification with Cybele produces. The preoccupation with her anxiety that renders the child unable to play or dream is lost in the fantasy of its privileged elevation.

Cybele is sometimes difficult to spot because she is socially so well adjusted. She's popular, chatty, and generally manages to sheathe her claws in her interactions. She's even likeable, effervescent and bubbly - until someone crosses or frustrates her secretly desperate need to identify sufficiently with another to keep at bay the panic of her insubstantial clay. Then her venomous vengeance is brought to bear on the poor unfortunate who can hardly believe the transformation taking place.

Cybele may even demonstrate considerable solicitousness of others' needs, but her motivation is suspect. She needs to gather fractured and damaged souls about her in order to detract from her own woundedness. Many therapists have a streak of this in them. They depend on their clients to manifest their own woundedness that can then be 'treated' at arm's length. Cybele is strongly attracted to the helping professions, and has close links with Apollo, the god of healing, but their relationship is clouded by her covert need to have in close proximity only those upon whom she can project her own neediness and fragmentation in order to feel solid and powerful once more.

 She gathers cripples about her, takes to her bosom the waifs and strays of the world. Everyone says how caring she is and indeed she is, until one of the waifs, like Attis, decides to go his or her own way. Then pour out the accusations of ingratitude, the emotional blackmail and the wheedling manipulations. With anything from an icy look or a dismissive gesture to the eternal damnation of the relationship, the Cybelian mother makes her displeasure vividly apparent. The Queen of Hearts in *Alice in Wonderland* comes to mind. The least infringement, the least show of autonomy, and it's 'off with her head'.

One of the most notorious incarnations of Cybele is in her role as mother-in-law. The attitude of the mother-in-law is legendary in its proportions. We have to make jokes about her in order to draw her sting and somehow contain the feelings she evokes. This role manages to unmask her so effectively because it is defined by that which she dreads most, the loss of her child and the sense of identity with which he provides her. Nowadays she usually manages to displace her aggression towards the would-be bride of her precious son, but even though it is the daughter-in-law who gets to feel the business end of the Cybelian mother's derision, it all starts with her possessiveness of her son and her feelings of abandonment and betrayal that his individuation evokes in her. The subtle sense of 'You aren't good enough for him, you're trespassing, he's mine', all starts with 'She can't give you what you need, only I know who you are. You are mine.'

Under such battle conditions, these sentiments must be diverted to the daughter-in-law in order to preserve the illusion of the good Mother. Any daughter-in-law knows full well that try as she might, she cannot win Cybele's favour. This is because Cybele's feelings and attitudes have nothing to do with her. It's not a personal thing. The relationship can only improve if Cybele takes her hooks out of her boy and lets him have his own life, an unlikely event if her power and identity are drawn from having him be her consort.

Of course, Midas, having witnessed Attis' fate, could always make a compromisingly poor choice of partner, marry unwisely and complain eternally about his wife which would at least gratify Cybele in the thought that despite his physical absence, he is at least still close to her in his heart. Many a poor marriage is sustained in such a fashion. The husband is confused about why he married this woman in the first place and why it is that now he's realised it's not working, he doesn't get out. The answer is often chillingly simple. Cybele's wrath at Midas' 'abandonment' is mollified when his every effort to live his own life ends in disaster.

Cybele is possessive, vengeful and exploitative. Any child is going to do whatever is necessary to remain safe from this aspect of the parent who has the power to invade it so completely. The child must avoid fulfilling its own potential with all urgency. It will do this passively by making poor marriages, bad career choices, failing to take opportunities, or it will actively get in trouble with the law, have 'accidents', or smash itself up in some way out of fidelity to this unspoken possessiveness on behalf of a parent who perceives her child as personal property and a means to her own unconscious gratification.

In order to escape the threat that Cybele hangs over its head the child makes sure it doesn't step out of line or get itself noticed in case it is ridiculed, shamed or hurt in some way. The child must make sure that it stifles its needs, and so, in essence, symbolically castrates itself, stills its voice and hides its light under a bushel to maintain the good favour of the parent.

A mother (or father) possessed by the archetype of Cybele cannot let the child have or be anything that the parent is not. The child must always be a pale shadow of the parent and must destroy any aspect of its character that would threaten to lend it even the vestiges of autonomy and individuality. The child grows up under a cloud of shame and doubt, shame that it feels to its very bones, and doubt that it is ever safe enough to let go of the eternal rounds of anxiety and paranoia that living in the twilight zone of Cybele's shadow engenders.

Interestingly enough, this sense that Cybele cannot allow the child anything that does not reflect the Mother's own being has mythic antecedents. According to a Phrygian myth recounted by Pausanias, Cybele was originally an hermaphrodite called Agdistis. Agdistis spontaneously sprang up from the earth when Zeus showered the slopes of Mount Didymus with his semen while he slept. The other Gods were thrown into a panic at the thought of what such a divine creature might be capable of and castrated Agdistis to prevent him/her from becoming too powerful. This being then grew up to be Cybele.

We can begin to appreciate Cybele's penchant for diverting her offspring from their own unfolding from this snippet of information. If a parent has been unable to react against her own disempowerment and injustice then she can only compulsively repeat the grievances committed against her. Parents can only justify the way that they were abused by calling it normal. If it is normal then this is the way to raise children and they are compelled to repeat the toxic patterns of poisonous pedagogy in order to still the cry of anguish from within that rises up in the face of man's inhumanity to man. In other words the parent abuses the child to dilute and ameliorate her own pain, enviously attacking the child's uniqueness in order to rationalise and explain away the manner in which she herself was enviously attacked.

Envy is part of life. It only becomes problematic when, for one reason or another, it is forced into the unconscious where it begins to create havoc and mayhem. Cybele has had to do this to conceal the memory of her own abuse and envious attack by the Olympians. This means that the normal feelings of envy that a Mother has for her baby cannot be moderated or governed in any way because she remains unaware that they exist. They are far too incompatible with the compensatory image of the 'Great Mother' that serves to repress the memory of being defiled as the child Agdistis.

Any mother is going to envy her baby. After all, the child has every need attended, is perpetually the focus of attention, need suppress none of its urges and only has to cry out to bring everyone running. In short it gets what it wants and family life revolves around it. The child's world may be far from perfection in actual fact, but compared to the parents' life it seems idyllic.

What could compare to 18 hours sleep and half a dozen feeds a day, the bliss of the breast and mother's arms? These envious feelings have to be processed by the parent. If they are made unconscious before this can happen out of the traumatic associations that the parent has to the consequences of envy, namely her own experience of abuse and disempowerment, then she will and indeed must direct her envious feelings toward the child in order to maintain the status quo in her own psyche.

If a child opts not to shoulder the burden of its parents' suffering then the parent has no barricade or defence against the authentic experience of her own childhood abuses. If either Attis or Midas escape Cybele's possessive need to live through them she will be forced to face the circumstances of her own attack by the Gods which will float back to the surface of consciousness of their own accord once she is deprived of the means to keep them at bay.

As the impending crisis and terrifying prospects of parental collapse begins to emerge, the child is left with the awful choice of either taking back up the yoke of suffering on its own shoulders and living out the parents' nightmare, or heaping up a great load of punishable guilt on its shoulders instead. Either way the child destroys itself. He cannot compound his fears with the possibility of them erupting direcly into his awareness. The threat of parental collapse on the one hand and the prospect of her envious attack on the other would be too much for him to bear. He has to maintain at least an image of the good-enough parent. So he hides from himself the source of this twofold horror. He places a veil of illusion over his true self whose impulse to autonomy and separateness threatens to reveal the dark force of the terrible mother and he places his own selfhood off-limits in order that the veil may continue to serve its purpose. He goes mad to stay sane.

Midas must never become himself. He must fail in every venture, and destroy all spontaneous manifestations of his true self. The source of his fears must not be identified, therefore they cannot be resolved. He must live with a kind of free-floating paranoia and live life both dangerously and destructively so that he can justify to himself the constant cloud of anxiety he is forced to live under. Paranoid and hogtied, Midas has at least kept his testicles; the irony of this consolation is that he must never use them, must never be potent or creative. He is in fact as much a eunuch as Attis, the only difference being that Attis knows it. For the sake of his comforting illusion Midas must stay within the orbit of Cybele's skirts, must divest himself of his power and independent will, and sabotage any opportunity that would truly test the fragile and shaky fantasy that he is his own man.

Few children, if any, can resist the seductive and heroic role of saving Cybele from her inner demons especially if they believe that their own needs will then be met in turn. This means that the child must ingest these demons himself, and become possessed by the impulse to fail, to implode, to rub himself out. Fritz Zorn, in his auto-biography *Mars*, (1981) in which he's quite clear that his cancer is a covert act of self-destruction, best expresses this feeling of being possessed by the parent:

I want to add one final item to this inventory of my life. My tragedy consists in this: I was not able to be and act out in my life what I feel to be the only worthwhile things in life. The reason I could not is that my own will and feelings and self were not the dominant forces in my life. It was the legacy of others that controlled me. What became of me was not what I wanted but what my parents implanted in me. My parents willed, for example, that sexuality would have no place in my life, even though, in that part of myself that I like to describe as 'my true self', I value sexuality above all else. I feel that only the very smallest part of myself is my true self. The greatest part of that self has been poisoned, violated, and destroyed by the hostile principle of which my parents were the most typical incarnation. What consumes me and what I suffer from is like an immense foreign body that is considerably larger than the part of myself I designate as 'my true self'. My soul has been invaded by 'my parents'.(Zorn 1982)

To realise the extent of the self-destructiveness that is entailed in maintaining the false compliant self that sanctions Cybele's invasion is more than most can bear. When life presents us with the opportunity of becoming more fully ourselves we simply have to pass it up, continue the rounds of self-destruction and, like Midas, make a complete mess of things. In the face of Dionysus' offer to wish for anything that he likes we can well imagine that Midas might feel considerable anxiety. The only way for him to deal with his dilemma is to ask for something that looks convincing to begin with but collapses before Cybele can descend upon him. He has to find some way of balancing out the conscious assumption that this is a great opportunity, with the unconscious fears of retribution should he be foolish enough to succeed in meeting his own needs.

Like Attis, Midas pre-empts Cybele's reaction by becoming the author of his own downfall. He foregoes his autonomy in an attempt to preserve it. He attempts to maintain some semblance of potency through his self-destruction. 'To consume oneself … prevents the possibility of being consumed by another' (Laing, ibid). His self-destruction becomes, ironically enough, a kind of insurance policy against Cybele's vengeance. By identifying with her and her destructiveness a little, Midas prevents her total invasion. Like a sovereign nation that concedes to the aggressor the annexation of a minor state, he prevents wholesale war from breaking out.

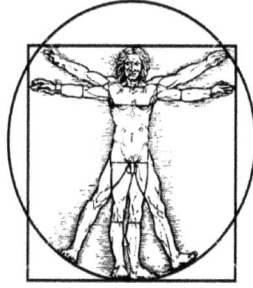

2
Gordius - the Absent Father

Not having a father is like not having a backbone.
Tom Pitt-Aikins

Midas' father was Gordius, the king who gave his name to the famous Gordian knot. This was an intricate and complicated knot with which Gordius tied up his chariot. Gordius vowed that he would give the entire Asian empire to whoever could unravel it. Many tried and failed. In the end Alexander the Great sliced through it with a single stroke of his sword. This was a somewhat liberal interpretation of the rules but it seemed that Gordius was in no mood to quibble and duly gave Alexander his reward. This left only the kingdom of Phrygia for Midas.

Why all this palaver with the knot? Why does Gordius not simply follow the normal and accepted rules of inheritance? We can only assume Gordius felt that Midas was in some way unfit to rule, that he was in fact disappointed in his son. The clue to this lies in the knot itself. Only the most cunning, the most heroic, the bravest, will resolve the problem of the knot, and only that man is fit to rule. Midas doesn't inherit because he is not a hero. He has failed to live up to his father's expectations. 'I'm not who I'm supposed to be', he says to himself. 'I'm letting them down by being me. I'm a failure.' The child begins to feel guilty, to blame and punish itself. 'If only I was like Alexander. If only I wasn't so stupid ...'

Gordius' need for the child to be larger than life, heroic, is the unconscious hope he harbours that this child will rescue him from the depression that his bursts of power are designed to mask. Gordius is afraid of power. He equates power with destruction rather than construction, and represses it in himself as a result. It explodes once in a while in an undifferentiated, wild kind of way, which further convinces him that power is bad. He compensates for this disowned power and the impotence it gives rise to with his grandiose knot, and the sense of superiority that this bestows on him.

Gordius' insecurity and the inauthenticity of his puffed up state is keenly felt by the child who begins to behave as though the fear of power were his own. 'Children', says analyst Frances

Wickes, 'gather from us the atmosphere of all that we most carefully ignore in ourselves. If our conscious goodness is founded on fear and repression, the atmosphere that we impart must be one of fear, restraint or insincerity … The unconscious of the child accepts responsibility for its solution' (Wickes 1955).

The powder keg of Gordius' fears regarding his own power are stowed away in Midas' secret self, where any attempt to take responsibility for them must blow up in the child's face. Unconscious contents have an instinct for the light. They have an inbuilt drive for re-integration and if they cannot achieve this in the generation they were born to, they'll try it in the next. Another way of saying this is that the child will always identify with the parent initially as a way of knowing itself. This identification is with the totality of the parent and not just the circumscribed image they present. 'The child is so much a part of the psychic atmosphere of the parents that secret and unsolved trouble between them … causes the child … to suffer from them as if they were its own troubles. It is hardly ever the manifest difficulty that has the poisonous effect [but] a disharmony repressed and neglected by the parents … that slowly pervade the child and destroy [its] security' (Wickes,ibid).

Gordius' failure to deal with the politics of power, substituting in its place the primitive pomp of the knot which abdicates him from the responsibility of exercising his power and his discrimination in a more conscious way, leaves Midas with a time bomb ticking away inside him. For reasons unknown he will always experience a strange yet indiscernible anxiety when called upon to exercise his power, either pushing away his responsibility, or using it recklessly and without due consideration, 'seized by wild furies of self-assertion' (Wickes, ibid), as with his foolish wish.

This puts me in mind of a young woman whose father was emotionally absent during her childhood and even more so from puberty onward, leaving her with a gap in her soul where a positive experience of fathering might have been lodged. This gap was filled up with ideal fantasies about the father, but also with a profound insecurity about the expression of her power which this vague shadowy figure embodied. His powerful absence evoked in her a sense of his mystique that bordered on unreality. Whenever this woman was called upon by circumstances to exercise her power or her discrimination she was overwhelmed with anxiety and a feeling of depersonalisation, of not being real. She was as profoundly passive in her therapy as she was in her life as a result, though I often wondered what her disowned power might be up to.

I found out one day when she suggested that she might resolve the trauma of a sexual violation by having me violate her in a similar way. When I expressed the opinion that this would only compound matters she flounced out of the room, never to be seen again, screaming at me that if I would not have sex with her then she'd find a therapist who would. Her power, kept so long under wraps for fear of its unmediated consequences, burst out in this florid instinctual manifestation of sexual manipulation that destroyed the therapeutic relationship and compelled her to withdraw from me as the father had withdrawn from her. His failure became her failure and his inability to address his own issues around power and sexuality left his daughter with a legacy that blew open her capacity to maintain intimate relations.

In retrospect the reaction of this woman was hardly surprising since the Gordian father's attitude towards the child is one that says 'if only you were different I could love you'. The child spends her life trying to fit the image expected of her, and understandably flies into an impotent rage when she discovers that it doesn't work. The father makes the daughter responsible for building the bridge between them but frustrates her every effort. In order to remain blind to his abuse of power she compulsively and destructively repeats the pattern of their relationship, having to imagine what's required by the other and having her fantasy frustrated. This way she can maintain the blaming of herself that is the father's implicit attitude towards her and have, if not a bridge, then at least a rope with which she unfortunately, but invariably, hangs herself.

Some psychoanalytic theory* actually protects the Gordian patriarch's unconscious abuse of power and sexuality, colluding with him by making the daughter responsible for her fantasy. This fails to take into consideration the parent's capacity for disowning the problematic feelings towards his attractive, innocent, virgin daughter, which then coalesce in the child's unconscious as a neurotic conflict of 'drives'. It would be easy to interpret what happens in our sessions as some aspect of an 'electra complex' but this would fail totally to see the deeper issues at stake, the desperate struggle of this woman to fulfil a task that was never hers in the first place. If the parent fails to address his sexuality, to acknowledge his power and the potency of his feelings, the daughter will live them out for him with disastrous consequences.

Gordius holds the child at arm's length out of the concern that his hollow core will become visible and undermine his shaky authority. He wants his depression redeemed but he's afraid to be found out, so he remains aloof - hovering on the edge of the child's vision, hoping that the magical purity of the child will thaw his frozen heart but unwilling to let it in that close even if such magic were possible. 'I always saw him as though through frosted glass,' said a woman of her Gordian father. 'He was there, but never really in the flesh. My biggest problem with him was that there was never a problem. There wasn't enough contact for problems to arise. For years I thought the lack of problems was because he was so wonderful. How I long to fight with him, to come to grips with the man.'

This was told me by a woman who destroyed all her relationships with her vicious temper, who fought substitute fathers all her life to try to make contact, to crack the frosted glass. She attacked men; she attacked life as well, 'I have to be perfect. Everything has to be 101 percent. I have to have goals and smash the goals.' But the goals, like her father, were always beyond her, she could smash neither the goals nor his frosted glass and so she felt like a permanent failure. Her need for 101 percent perfection led her to her worst nightmare - imperfection and failure. She failed to rescue him from his depression and failed to live her life in the process because she couldn't bear to be ordinary, couldn't bear the impotence of having him be forever beyond her reach. So she was forever trying to transcend herself, forever hurting herself in the attempt, forever destroying the 'merely human' aspect of herself that she blamed for not being able to create a relationship with her father, a task that was never hers to initiate in the first place. He denied his responsibility, lost the authority that went with it, and induced in his daughter a total foundering of the ability to relate to men.

Gordius is a weak man. It shows in his choice of such an overpowering woman as Cybele for a wife. He makes himself look strong and complicated, like his knot, but it's all a front. His authority is not his own but that of the crown, the collective opinion bestowed on him to rule that he claims by right rather than by any natural ability inherent in the man himself. Gordius can only sustain this power to rule, or the power to father for that matter, by wielding power, by using his power not to support or to nurture but to withhold, to humiliate, to mock and to disown.

When he is confronted by genuine authority in the form of Alexander who simply slices through his knot, Gordius collapses like a house of cards. Such a man only has authority in so far as he is given it on trust by others or in so far as he takes it from them in the same way that he deprives Midas of his inheritance. Though he judges Midas as incompetent and weak, berating and punishing him for appearing to be so; he also needs him to look weak so that he may puff himself up by comparison. We can imagine for instance, that the fame of his knot gives him great renown though it is of course, all at the expense of Midas' impoverishment, disinheritance and the rationalising rumour of the son's incompetence that everyone, including Midas, has come to believe. Midas cannot mourn his father's distance or diminishment of him, but has to find a way of justifying and promoting his own demise. He creates a link with the father by fulfilling Gordius' negative expectations.

This is very different from the self-destructiveness that results from the child's interaction with Cybele, but no less effective in its impact. Here, the self-destructiveness serves as a defence against the parent's absence rather than its invasion and is characterised primarily by guilt rather than anxiety or paranoia.

Midas can never reach the idealistic vision set in place for him by Gordius. There is no point in trying since every effort will fail and heap shame upon his head. The only way out is for the child to plead guilty as charged in order, at least, to preserve the protective authority of his father by colluding with Gordius' system of values. He is a failure. He is guilty. All that remains is just punishment.

"As long as I struggle between my desire to be independent and strong and my feelings insignificance and powerlessness I am caught in a tormenting conflict. If I succeed in reducing myself to nothing ... I may save myself." (Fromm 1947)

The easiest way to do this is in relation to an apparently powerful other who will ensure the uniform suppression of individual impulses to be oneself. Isolation and anxiety are escaped through submission to an authority other than one's own. This, however, is humiliating. The only way to avoid such humiliation is by renewed identification with the aggressor. To preserve this identification and the sense of power, control and superiority it bestows, the individual must perpetuate the punishment of his true self. In other words he must destroy himself in order not to become conscious of the painful fact that he is destroying himself. He goes mad to stay sane.

Self-destruction is essential to preserving this myth of there being a dominant authority 'out there' that is unambiguously in our favour, whose sole purpose is our succour and nurture.

Bob, a long-standing client in therapy, describes the urge to 'go out like an incandescent flash'. I ask what this would give him. He is quite clear - it would stop the incessant feelings of guilt and give him 'a ticket to the family circle'. Years of alcohol and heroin abuse have served to keep his ticket valid. To be excluded from this circle is tantamount to death, if not physical then spiritual and emotional. Bob will strike any bargain including the disavowal of his own authority in order to get into the circle and then forget what he has done. All he is aware of is the urge to drink himself into a stupor, or get stoned, or destroy himself in some way to atone for his guilt.

This guilt, and the self-destructive condemnation that goes with it, are necessary to the smooth running of the family machinery. 'Guilt', says Terry Pratchett, (1990) 'is the grease in which the wheels of authority turn.' So, if the father of the circle maintains himself by competing with his son and continually 'winning', the son must see the competition as normal and good and continually lose. He grows up having to compete and having to lose. The prospect of actually winning a competition - getting that job, winning that girl, sends him into a paroxysm of guilt and depression.

All this is thrown sharply into focus by an unexpected and impromptu award Alan is given at a company dinner. Suddenly he's 'made it'. All around him are lights, people clapping, beaming chairman proffering a silver trophy. This should be the peak of his career, but inside all he feels is a sense of utter desolation, emptiness, feeling of failure and an unnameable guilt. 'It shouldn't be me. This belongs to someone else.' By association, the celebration of his own authority is what has always served to have him excluded. So he reaches for the bottle or even less consciously crashes his car. He can only be successful if he fails, only sane if he's mad. If he fails, loses or becomes neurotic then he is seen to uphold the family myth that sanctifies his inclusion.

The route back into the absent father's affections is to prove him right in his opinions. This will at least create some congruency, some fulfilment of the longing for contact and approval. For Midas this means confirming Gordius' opinion that he is unfit to rule, and so he must heap upon himself low self-worth, abject and miserable consideration of his own being, one blunder after another.

An unholy communion is better than no communion at all. This travesty can only be held in place by actively, if unconsciously, searching for ways to run oneself down, seeking and destroying the shattered remnants of soul that might have escaped being lacerated by the father's dismissive flail. In this way Midas finds a perverse route, the only route, back into Gordius' affections, and some place, albeit a dunghill, to call himself his father's son.

Charles, another young man, describes his feelings of worthlessness as 'sacred'. Despite the great burden of this worthlessness, it seems to have great value. I ask him to expand. 'Well', he says, 'if I were actually to go to my Father and knock on the door and say to him "you were right, I am worthless", and prove I believe it by doing all these things to myself as punishment

… well, he would be vindicated and exonerated.' 'And if he were vindicated and exonerated …?' I ask. 'Well', says Charles with tears in his eyes, 'he might love me then, mightn't he?'

One of the most heart-rending and tragic accounts of just how extensively the vicarious abuse of paternal authority can undermine the unfolding sense of the child's own purpose and drive it onto the rocks of self-destruction in order to allay its guilty 'failure', is to be found in Hermann Hesse's *The Prodigy*.(1957)

Hans is the tale's youthful hero who can never quite gain the unconditional approval of his father or the myriad authorities that represent the various arms of the patriarchal state despite his great intelligence and scholastic ability. Teachers, principals, clergymen, preachers: all have made it their duty, a point of personal 'honour' to instil in the prodigy their own special mark. This can only be done by covertly breaking Hans, by crushing the 'dangerous flame' of his own authority, a flame that must be 'extinguished and stamped out'. Hans has to collude, he must believe that it is all for his own good and drives himself to exhaustion believing that it is his own will rather than theirs that fuels his inevitable collapse in the desperation to be his father's Alexander.

Hans dreams of being force-fed food that he hates and that his spirited but banished friend, Hielner, who represents the voice of his true self, is dead, dead and carried away on a bier by the aforementioned authorities. Exhausted and depleted he relinquishes the special place at theological college that is slowly killing him and finds that this last effort to save himself is met with summary dismissal and abandonment. 'He had ceased to be a vessel into which all manner of things could be stuffed, a field to be sown with a variety of seeds: it was no longer rewarding to spend time and trouble on him …' (ibid) Still Hans is oblivious to what is happening. He is conscious only 'of his disappointed father whose hopes he had betrayed'. So little of his own authority remains intact that even his suicide is almost an accident.

The father's ideal is unattainable since it is, after all, a compensatory fantasy for the father's own feelings of inferiority and nothing to do with the child's psychology. The only recourse to alleviate the father's feelings about himself is to fail utterly and thus to raise the father up by comparison. He embodies the father's unconscious feelings of failure so that the father may be free of them. If he cannot redeem the father by being the Alexandrian hero he does it by being his father's anti-hero.

For Midas to release himself from this psychological serfdom would be to threaten the security of his final remaining bond to Gordius as well as to reveal it for the miserly piece of self-deprecation that it is. Even more, it would throw into the light that terrible longing for approval which allows a child to sink to such depths unawares. This cannot be allowed. The foolish wish to turn things into gold confirms the Father's derisive opinion that he's incompetent to rule. It reinforces the negative emotional equity that is Midas' sole remaining link to Gordius, the only defence he has against a despair of unbridgeable longing, and plugs up tight the emptiness of an unhallowed heart.

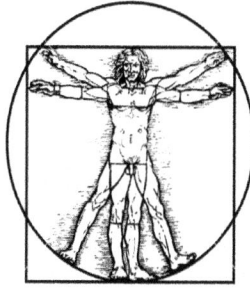

3
Self-Hatred: a Legacy

Self-aggression can always be sure of its victim!
F. Perls

The awful contradiction in expectations that Gordius and Cybele have of their son, coupled with the utterly polarised views that each parent holds of Midas, threaten to tear him in two. He cannot succeed in the eyes of one parent without damning himself in the eyes of the other.

Gordius relates to Midas as a failure. Cybele relates to him as a personal hero saviour. Gordius uses his authority to dismiss, Cybele uses hers to possess. Gordius withholds his blessing because Midas has fallen short precisely in those realms that Cybele demands that he must fail, in his autonomy and individuality. Gordius is cold and disinterested, utterly dismissive of Midas' fate except that he should disinvest Gordius of his depression and low self-esteem. Cybele is the opposite, hysterical and invasive, holding the threat of her wrath over Midas should he have any aspiration towards his own independence, crushing his free spirit with her neediness and anxiety.

If Midas embodies the hero demanded of him by Gordius with its connotations of personal mastery, ingenuity and leadership, those qualities personified by the transcending spirit of Alexander, he must betray Cybele whose covert injunction it is that he live life in her service. If he renounces his independence and personal potency in order to kindle his Mother's affections then he fails in Gordius' eyes and earns only his father's contempt. Midas is caught in a trap. His true self is not only under attack but also caught in crossfire. His only hope is to internalise this crossfire and to make of his soul a battlefield where the remnants of his own authority are firmly trampled into the irreconcilable mud of a profoundly self-destructive neurosis.

Midas must find some way of containing the contrary expectations of Gordius and Cybele, as well as the authentic but dangerous feelings the child finds surfacing inside. He can manage this very well if he deadens his humanity and turns himself into a kind of mechanical toy. The degree to which this phenomenon is true for modern children of Phrygian parents never ceases to amaze me. The frequency with which persons of such parents describe themselves as toys, dolls, zombies, androids, robots, cyborgs or puppets, is very high. Perhaps this is because depersonalisation of oneself is such a catch-all solution to the problems that face the child in such a hostile and controlling environment. A male client of 30 described the poetry of his robotic adaptation as follows. 'Well, it killed several birds with one stone. As a robot, I could be superhuman for Mother, subhuman for father and distance myself from my feelings all at the same time.'

To become a robot is to destroy one's humanity, but it also prevents total disintegration. It's a madness that paradoxically defends against insanity. To some degree we all have a tendency to dehumanise ourselves even if this is only manifested by the desire to be statistically 'normal'. The more potent the effects of Gordius and Cybele, however, the more it becomes imperative to destroy the unique human quality of life to reduce oneself to a thing, to have one's worth become contingent on behaviour rather than on one's being.

The Phrygian child is required to perform and to provide an impossible service. This the robot personality achieves very well. By depersonalising itself, the child retains some vestiges of autonomy and control. It pre-empts parental demands to be both more and less than itself, contains the emptiness, pain, and fear of disintegration within a hard shell of robot armour without having to acknowledge the nature of its innards or the purpose of such protection. Like Frankenstein's monster, the robot personality generalises his feeling of hatred and envy towards the whole world in order to preserve an ideal relationship with his parents who are his 'makers', and having given him life, owe him nothing further.

The effect of either Phrygian parent is sufficient to destabilise Midas' sense of self. Together they form a cocktail so toxic that Midas must poison himself by degrees in order to build up sufficient psychological tolerance to prevent the parental draught from doing him in without remorse. Essential to this process is the perversion of his own intrinsic being. He must go mad in order to preserve himself from the reality that he is adrift in a sea of madness. This can only be achieved by consistently undermining and destroying the natural authority within himself that testifies to the impossibleness of his situation. He retreats into himself leaving behind a pseudo-personality that can only respond mechanically and prescriptively to his environment.

The child sacrifices his integrity to keep the family together and the atmosphere within it bearable. He disintegrates so that the family doesn't have to. This desperate need to hold the family together engenders a rage against becoming himself with all its feared and imagined consequences. In what amounts to a Herculean effort to retain the parents' conflict within himself so that he can achieve the miracle of identifying with both of them despite their opposition he at least creates the promise of a familiar and stable existence.

Midas' self-destructiveness is an indispensable means of treading the thin line between the engulfment of merging with Cybele and the isolation of Gordius' abandonment. Both engulfment and isolation are totally outside the child's control, experiences of utter powerlessness and impotence. Self-destructiveness at one and the same time affirms that a self is at least experiencing something, something between nothingness and unbearable intensity as well as providing a common focus of concern for his otherwise wildly disparate parents.

In the meantime Midas also has to reconcile himself to the authentic feelings of his true self at having his integrity mocked in this way. In order to consolidate his increasingly precarious situation he has to find some way of dealing with the feelings evoked at having to erect this false, compliant facade of himself. He's bound to experience considerable hostility towards the objects of his frustration. But the precious relationships have already been dealt a crucial blow so his hatred must be hidden. His grip on reality is mortgaged to the hilt, and any expression of his true feelings would bring the edifice tumbling down, plunging him into psychological insolvency.

These feelings cannot be expressed so they must be impressed. Aggressive energy has to go somewhere and if the environment or the family cannot support the expression of 'negative' emotions they will be turned against himself. 'In this way', says Freud (1955), 'an object (outer) loss is transformed into an ego (inner) loss and the conflict between the ego and the loved person turned into an (internal) cleavage.' The idealisation of the parents can be preserved and the pain of both abandonment and invasion kept at bay – by attacking and turning his anger in on himself.

One of the most pernicious forms that this can take is Midas' now burgeoning hatred of himself that, though it may not be manifest as overt acts of self-destruction, nevertheless pervades his life in any number of apparently insignificant little ways. Midas is less conscious of his self-hatred than he might be if he found himself explicitly damaging himself. This however does not prevent passive expressions of self-hatred seriously undermining and destroying his life. In a myriad number of situations his self-hatred debases and corrupts him. He puts himself down, subserviates himself, fails to express his needs, allows himself to be walked over by powerful others and sabotages his own calling with a continuous daily plunder of both his worth and esteem.

He has learnt that in order to be loved he must be other than himself and so the full force of his hatred 'prompted by the dread of what might happen if one were to be oneself in actuality' (Laing. 1960), is brought to bear on that authentic part of him which seems to be the source of all the trouble. He must actively, if covertly, seek out justification for his clandestine attack on himself and finds it in a great heap of secret beliefs that he is a failure, that he deserves nothing, that he has no rights and nothing to offer.

Midas might puff himself up a bit, and strut around like Gordius. Alternatively he will be protesting his weakness like Cybele, but judging and hating himself for it, holding it up like a curse, quite unable to reach that part of himself with compassion. The longing for wholeness that it represents cannot be heard. Midas' antagonistic campaign against himself has silenced its voice.

Through his self-hatred, Midas has become his own rival. His rejection of himself produces opposing factions within him, each hell bent on the other's demise. Like a pair of Mafioso twins or a latter day Cain and Abel they exact their vendetta upon one another, true and false selves locked in mortal combat. Such a pyrrhic battle both generates self-hatred and feeds off it, the widening gyre of its spiralling circle compels new allegiances into its service on psychological territory previously untouched by the hand of battle, until the entire psyche is plunged into trench warfare, a poisoned and barren land presided over by Gods that seem to be as caught in the bickering antipathies as the soldiers of fortune themselves.

Such internal warfare, the clanging of confusion and conflict, soon saps Midas' strength. He becomes sullen, sarcastic and snaps at others when he thinks he can get away with it. He's listless, depressed, bored, moody. The only thing he's really passionate about is his secret self-loathing which he must fuel sufficiently to make at least something felt through the sodden eiderdown of his depression, something to remind him that he's alive. His self-hatred feeds his depression as well as providing light relief from it, requiring more and more vitriol to be heaped on his head to keep the growing cloud of doom from descending, or the true voice of his silenced soul from being heard.

On the surface of things Midas might preoccupy himself with how loathsome the outside world is, how unjust or ungrateful are his people or the neighbouring heads of state. Yet beneath it all he berates himself for not being a good enough king or for not being sufficiently heroic to have all of Asia Minor or for failing to have the courage to dispense with Alexander and his cohort of petty despots. The irony of his situation is that Midas needs to hate himself in order to remain adequately preoccupied with his internal struggle not to notice the extent of his self-destruction, and yet it is precisely his self-hatred that he unconsciously refers to in order to justify the covert rounds of self-destruction and missed opportunity.

Archie watches his front door close behind him. He knows the keys are inside. He also knows he has time to reach the door and stop it slamming shut and locking him out, but he lets it go - impassively watching as it swings too – knowing the aggravation it will cause, but he can't help himself. He stands rooted to the spot, cursing himself and the world which simply treats him as he treats himself and watches as the door clicks shut.

Archie talks about this 'scuppering' of himself, knows he does the same thing in any number of different arenas of his life, situations in which he feels equally powerless to help himself and realises that this despising of himself serves a very useful purpose. 'First I sink myself and then I go over to the promontory from which everyone is watching me flounder and slag myself off for being such an idiot. They all join in, of course, it's like a moment of togetherness.' This togetherness cuts through his depression for a time, but then gathers weight from this latest self-betrayal and soon he's sunk even further into the mire of his self-hatred.

Sean dreams of murder, the murder of something faceless and voiceless within himself. We had been speaking the previous week of his hatred of supermarkets to which his Cybelian Mother would drag him as a prop for her paranoid anxieties. It was easier to hate the neutral supermarket than the object of his frustration at being so invaded by her neediness and helpless posturing, but in the process that hate which not even the largest and busiest supermarket can contain spills back on his own soul where he silently murders himself in his dreams.

Paul speaks reasonably and with conciliation of a lover that has led him a great song and dance of betrayal. Despite the abuse, the blaming and the contempt with which he's been treated he remains impassive. It's 'not Christian' to feel any anger or hatred. So his unchristian feelings stay locked in his own breast where he treats himself like an infidel and covertly invites the world to follow suit.

None of this self-hatred is instinctual or 'internally derived' (Greenberg & Mitchell, 1983) it is as a result of 'thwarted love' (Suttie, 1935). Where there is love the outward expression of hate can be tolerated; where there is not, hate is held in and used to attack the true self which is blamed for the loved one's absence or ambivalence.

Hatred is a necessary part of life. It helps us know who we are by first establishing what we are not. Without hate life becomes sentimental, boundaries and identity get mushy. We fear hatred, particularly our own because it's incompatible with our self-image and because we equate hate with damage. The irony is that conscious hate, entering into the actual experience of hate, liberates us from its possession. We have it, it does not have us. Because we have it we can mediate its expression in a way that can never be when the experience of hate is kept unconscious. Unlike the sense of separation and increased sense of identity that conscious hate can bring, unconscious hatred aimed at oneself creates divisiveness and self-alienation.

Most of us are afraid that our hate will cause damage and of course it does, to the facade of things-as-we'd-like-them-to-be. It wrecks our idealisations, dis-illusions the romantic sentimental fantasy of how-things-used-to-be and confronts us with deeper realities that are incommensurable with our images of ourselves, implicitly asking us disturbing questions. What is this? Where did it come from? What does it mean? The experience of a more authentic self, damages relationships as well, in so far as it damages the narrow limits within which we are compelled to experience them. We might lose a few friends into the bargain or become more distant in our family relationships. This seems bleak but the alternative is worse. We have no real choice about whether we hate or not. The choice is only how we hate, whether we can tolerate hate's proximity enough to keep it on a leash, to prevent it from roaming too freely the halls of our own souls.

Our fear is that hate destroys love. Midas cannot contain opposites. It must be either love or hate, one or the other. The irony is that if only he were a little less sentimental about his life then Midas might find that his hatred need not be experienced to the detriment of his love. He might even find that it gives him the capacity to love, particularly to love himself without which love of others is virtually impossible. Hatred makes love possible because hate itself is 'love grown angry' (Guntrip, 1968).

The experience of hate sustains and preserves us, gives the individual a sense of identity and self-value. Hatred always has a context. 'I hate you because of what you have done to me.' The individual hates because he feels abused or cheated or wronged. Implicit in this experience is the sense that the individual deserves better because he is worth more. This sense of being worth something more is the belief about oneself out of which loving and accepting love depend.

Hatred might be the only way the individual has left to express his worth or the validity of his own subjective experience. When this hatred is turned inwards the last line of defence preserving the sovereignty of one's own separateness and autonomy is broached. The person becomes no more than a trustee in an alien world, an exile in one's own land. Disintegration and loss of self is complete. Hatred prevents this inner disintegration from happening. It attacks the identification with others that prevents individuation from occurring, which is why it is the feeling above all others that the child of Cybele must repress. This is not because hate is intrinsically bad or any worse than any other feeling, but because it is the emotion par excellence that creates separation, the one thing that threatens Cybele's secret dependency.

Hatred says, 'I am not you, I cannot live your life or die your death'. Hatred confirms the self and the inherent right to autonomy and self-preservation. Hatred creates boundaries which in turn delineate identity, separating out me from not-me. This is indispensable to the child of a Cybelian mother who co-opts all and sundry into her shaky world to bolster its uncertain frame. It is to preserve its selfhood that the child must learn to hate, insofar as hate is part of its authentic reality. When appropriately channelled, hate is a great fount of energy and internal coherence for the psyche, but when the object of hatred is one's own self, the power source, like a nuclear reactor, goes into a state of meltdown, polluting and defiling the surrounding land it had previously served with light and heat, turning it into a wasteland where the soul can no longer flourish or spread its roots.

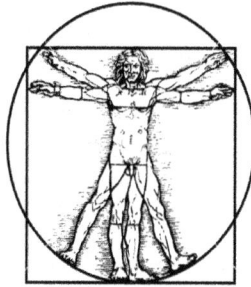

4
The Need for Greed

The woes of Midas which his greedy wish ensued
Marked for derision to all future times.
Dante

This turning back on himself of authentic hate is not the only inadvertent consequence of Midas self-destructive family legacy. There is also the bottomless pit of unmet needs within him that his subsequent idealisations of Gordius and Cybele have left unattended. This now becomes a source of self-destruction in its own right. Despite the comforting illusions of the safely tailored world he's come to inhabit, Midas is left with a feeling of unbearable emptiness, a slough of despond that no amount of effort on his part can redress alone. This emptiness cannot be dealt with in the same way as the authentic but unacceptable feelings that Midas has so neatly squirrelled away. In fact his emptiness is the direct result of having had to excise the genuine contents of his inner world.

Emptiness can only be filled up; and if the void within cannot be ameliorated by acknowledging and mourning the reality of its existence then the child is propelled into the futile effort of filling it up some other way. Gold, gold and more gold will be poured into the terrible hole in his psyche that cannot be named but nevertheless impresses its desperation upon him with renewed and never ending craving.

The unbounded greed that results can never be sated since the object of his desire has been displaced. No amount of chocolate pudding is going to speak to the need for affection. No amount of corporate takeovers is going to fulfil the need for personal potency. No amount of narcosis can dream away the hollow ache, though it may distract and seduce or terrify sufficiently to confuse the issue long enough for a moment's reprieve.

The self-destructiveness that invariably follows on the heels of this despairing but unconscious compulsion to fill up the void of empty longing is quite unintentional and different from the impulse to hobble himself that's designed to maintain contact with the parent. It is, however, no less harmful for that. It becomes so pressing that the warnings of danger which are normally available get completely ignored. The addict injects himself regardless. The bulimic binges and purges unheedful of the body's demise. That desperation to fill up one's emptiness, by whatever means possible, disregards the now muted protests of reason.

Greed is the symbolic craving to have back what we once gave away and continue to give away of ourselves in order to keep the peace. It is not just the craving for simply what we do not have or were not given. It is also the result of maintaining a status quo whose object it is to lessen the anxiety created by the experience and expression of being a whole person. Greed is both the craving for, and the avoidance of our wholeness; hence our conflict, desperation and misery. The irony and despondency of the Midas syndrome begin to emerge. In order to be whole, to have a sense of self, he must have more. Not X amount, but more, to try to fill the hole that threatens to swallow him up from within; but nothing can slake the thirst, emptiness, boredom and depression it was meant to gratify.

Greed may be born of the genuine attempt to experience oneself as whole, but it is fated to produce the opposite. It makes of oneself an object in a world of objects to be consumed and alienated in the same way as the object of one's greed itself. The experience of living becomes one of being drained, of having to be on guard. Death and destruction assume a greater reality than life and growth. To come to a point of satiation and contentment is always beyond attainment because one must constantly become more powerful, more aggressive. In fact, ' … in a world of unlimited desires the strife would have to continue even under circumstances of absolute abundance' (Fromm, 1942).

If Midas acknowledges the true source of his hungering, it would entail the collapse of his inauthentic adaptation which he imagines is his true self. This means that his greed can only be put paid to by facing an experience of annihilation. Thus his greed, despite its self-destructive character, must be held onto and promoted at all costs. We too institutionalise greed and have built a culture around it despite its irreverence for the soul's needs. We make a constitutional right of the 'pursuit of happiness'. We dress our greed up as 'the competitive spirit' or 'free market economy', which is just a fancy way of saying that greed is not only good, but good business.

In order that consumer society and the compulsive sentiments that drive it do not become dirty words we have needed a respectable theory of human nature to justify, account for, and obscure the philosophy of greed that underpins it. This ideology must enable society to perceive its sickness in terms of health, its destruction in terms of progress and its created evil in terms of natural necessity. This is so well put by Alice Miller that she deserves to be quoted in full:

Every ideology offers its adherents the opportunity to discharge their pent up affect (aggression, greed, addictive craving) collectively while retaining the idealised primary object (civilisation, progress, democracy). This ideology sanctions or even encourages the forbidden feelings which the individual will finally be able to live out in a collective framework (consumer society).

It should, then, be no surprise to us that, at the dawn of our society's 'golden' era, when consumer values were becoming sacrosanct, when money and machines were becoming more important than those they served, and when Europe was consolidating the military expansionism that dominated the world, an innate psychic structure justifying greed should be 'discovered' by Freud. He called it the Pleasure Principle. 'It seems that our entire psychical activity is bent on procuring pleasure … and that this is automatically regulated' (Freud, 1955). This principle is ascribed 'dominance over the course of the processes of mental life', which means that we are inherently motivated by lust and greed.

The effect of this pernicious ideology is to rationalise greed and the consumer values it serves so that we need not look any deeper at the emptiness and loneliness it is covertly intended to obscure. When the pleasure principle is given autonomous status in the psyche by Freud it is also given moral value by society in the form of the 'pursuit of happiness'. We fail to realise that the pursuit of pleasure (as opposed to the enjoyment of it when it happens along) is a compensatory mechanism attempting to redress the existential emptiness of life. This it cannot do, or at least, not for long.

In the attempt to prevent himself from realising the failure of his gold-making to provide his life with meaning, Midas can only re-immerse himself with renewed vigour into the very system that is creating his pain, isolation and loneliness. In so doing he becomes even more removed from that which might redeem him, and correspondingly more desperate in his pursuit of its insufficient substitutes. Like salt water to a man in thirst he becomes even more dehydrated, his condition even more urgent and yet still he sips at that which is his undoing.

We, like Midas, are having to learn the hard way. We pursue our veiled doctrines of greed with all sincerity only to find that, not only are we still empty at the end of the day, but that we have also succeeded in further destroying both ourselves and our environment into the bargain. We fail to notice this because we must fail to notice it. It's not that people don't care, but that the preservation of themselves and their planet is in fact secondary to the maintenance of private myths about life and existence that bear little resemblance to reality but are nevertheless preferable to the truth.

 We are compelled to destroy both our humanity and our planet for as long as we kid ourselves that our wellbeing is more important to us than polishing the images of ourselves which feed on both our collective resources and our personal integrity. We do this in order to fill the gaping maw of that cavernous void within which the least lapse of compulsive grasping is liable to reveal for what it is, the painful loss of self, an inner emptiness born of betrayal by both ourselves and others which we feel so powerless to address that we will destroy ourselves in order not to have to notice it.

This is the Midas syndrome in full spate. Having placed our values outside ourselves where they alternately frustrate and gratify us, we incur upon our increasing fragile sense of self a desperation for something solid to clutch onto that is ever beyond our reach. Our secret war against our own souls demands that we destroy the only abiding values, the only meaning, that cannot be eroded by time or eternity in which there might be at least some reconciliation with arbitrary death, cosmic insecurity and the fickleness of a fundamentally ambiguous universe. To hide from what we have done we set about nature, both our personal nature and nature as a whole, as if it were an object of extreme hatred. We obsessively cast golden calves, irrespective of the expense, to keep at bay our unwittingly perpetuated emptiness and the cry of the self that echoes up and down its long, lonely corridors.

Let's now return to the story itself in more detail, where we find King Midas on the eve of his golden wish and the threshold of a strange encounter.

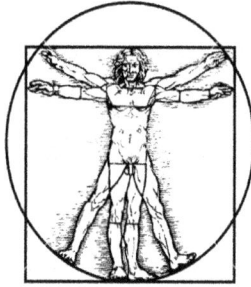

5

The Seduction of Paradise

The charmed sunset, linger'd low adown
In the red west thro' mountain clefts the dale
Was seen far inland, and the yellow down
Bordered with palm, and many a winding vale
And meadow set with slender galingale;
A land where all things always seemed the same!
Tennyson: The Lotus Eaters

One day King Midas was out walking in the hills of his native Phrygia. Along the way, he accidentally stumbled across the sleeping form of Silenus, tutor of Dionysus, who had strayed away from the nearby camp of the dark god. True to form, the old man had drunk himself into a stupor.

Silenus was a comical figure, overweight, bald, with bright red cheeks and a snub nose. He was permanently drunk but he was also immensely wise. He had endless stores of knowledge, could prophesy the future and would reveal the destiny of anyone who succeeded in tying him up during the heavy slumber that followed his drinking bouts.

Despite his appearance, Silenus was a great prize to discover. He had parentage among the Gods, some saying his father was Hermes, messenger of the Gods, and his Mother, Gaia, the Earth. Others said that he was born of the blood of Uranus after Cronos had mutilated him.

Whatever was true, Silenus had considerable divine powers and we can well imagine Midas' excitement and his desire to take advantage of the old drunkard's promise of prophecy. Once he had woken Silenus, Midas asked him to share his wisdom. Silenus then told him the following story:

Once upon a time there were two cities outside the world called Eusebes, the city piety, and Machimus, the city of war. The inhabitants of Eusebes were always happy and died laughing. Those of Machimus were born fully armed and spent their lives fighting. Both sets of people were very rich. They decided to come and visit our world and arrived in the land of the Hyperboreans. When they saw the miserable conditions of the Hyperboreans and learnt that these were the Earth's happiest people they returned to their own lands in despair.

Midas is disturbed by Silenus' response, he doesn't understand and assumes that the old man is still drunk. Silenus gets to his feet and the two make their way back to Dionysus' camp.

What can we make of this piece of the tale? How are we to understand Midas' 'chance' discovery and the strange prophecy that follows? Let's begin with the figure of Silenus himself. We can learn much about him from his parentage. You might feel that there is a contradiction in the two different accounts of his birth, but these begin to disappear if we look closer. As the son of Hermes and Gaia he is the product of opposites, instability, change and impermanence on the one hand and grounded solidity on the other. He stands between opposites without being crushed by the contradiction. Hermes was messenger of the Gods to men and also mediated between Hades and Olympus. We might expect the fruit of his union with Gaia to embody a particularly direct and grounded form of wisdom. His special role is that he stands between the opposites of consciousness and the unconscious, conveying messages across the divide. As son of Gaia he is likely to do this in an instinctual way, his messages are going to be earthy and to the point.

The other version of Silenus' birth actually captures a similar idea. Cronos castrated his father Uranus in order to separate him from Gaia, with whom he was joined, in order that the world could be formed. Cronos pushed apart the sky from the earth and Silenus was born from their instinctual union. He was formed between the opposites, and in this case not just that of sky and earth but also of time, represented by Cronos and eternity represented by Uranus who was the first of the Gods to be born out of primordial chaos.

The paradisial land of Hyperborea that Silenus refers to is a metaphor for the idealised life that Midas has been living. The Hyperboreans live in a mythic land 'beyond the north wind', that is, beyond the sufferings of winter with which the north wind was associated. The people here live simple unreflective lives that lend their existence the appearance of eternal peace and happiness.

The harsh realities of the real world do not obtrude upon the Hyperborians who are more than content to live naively and without the complication of those poor souls who live beyond their protective borders. Time stands still in Hyperborea. The climate and the season are ever the same. When the people themselves begin to change and age, they throw themselves off high cliffs rather than face the prospect of old age, the realities of the human condition or anything else that might taint their innocent world view.

At first glance Hyperborea looks like a land of milk and honey, but there is no birth of consciousness here and it all ends in self-destruction. The unified opposites of the true self, represented by the people of Eusebes and Machimus, are appalled, and retreat back into the unconscious. As a result, the people of Hyperborea remain naive, living in a world of unreal fantasy where they remain unworked by the eroding yet transformative blasts of the north wind.

Silenus is trying to warn Midas of the consequences of subscribing to his idealistic and distorted vision of the world. He is pointing to the inevitable self-destruction inherent in the maintenance of the false self, attractive though it may seem. Withdrawal into Hyperborea is a retreat into paradisial childhood in the attempt to heal one's wounds. But if the wound cannot be named it cannot be dressed either. Midas is thus compelled to inhabit this naive state of mind without deriving any healing benefit while still remaining open to the luring threat of the high cliffs.

Midas has had to repress the painful circumstances of his childhood. In their place he erects an idealised fantasy to defend against the unpleasant realities of his life. No doubt he sees Gordius' giving Asia Minor to Alexander as just, and feels proud of his father's clever scheme with the knot. Perhaps he brags about it to his friends, telling then how wise his father is and what a great king he must be. Likewise, he holds his Mother in the highest respect, managing to explain away her moody instability. He describes her viciousness as 'spirited', her possessiveness he calls 'protective' and her attack on Attis he puts down to some fault on behalf of his half-brother whose loss he no doubt feels was 'for his own good'. All this defensive idealisation means that the potential for self-destructiveness is firmly locked in place and it is this that Silenus' prophecy intends to reveal.

Idealising one's past in order not to have to face the reality of it has a pernicious effect on self image. It is not simply a question of calling good what was bad. In order to really believe it all, those aspects of the self which disagree must be eliminated, leaving the person with a thoroughly circumscribed perception of himself that must compliment the distorted fantasy he has of the family. The child then has to live up to this image and inevitably winds up either over-reaching and destroying himself or falling short of the desired image and beating himself up for 'failing'. The child can't win. Whichever way it goes his paradise results in self-destruction.

Our idealisations of both who we are and where we have come from serve to allay the anxiety of being profoundly unsure of either. They provide us with a simple, uncomplicated view of life that permits us to live with surety and conviction. They have a deep internal consistency, that acts as a scaffold to the wobbling sense of self that is the child's legacy from Gordius and Cybele. Life might well be blinkered, but blinkers have a purpose, they prevent the horse from excessive sensory input that threatens to frighten and overwhelm it. Here, however, the analogy ends. The horse is not prevented from becoming himself. He remains himself despite the blinkers because he knows that the blinkers are there. We are different. We forget that the blinkers are on and take what we see to be an accurate reflection of the world.

We might feel that this transparent fantasy Midas subscribes to, one in which he must destroy himself to preserve his rapid vision of unreality, is hardly worth the suffering entailed in keeping it afloat. But the poetry of it all is that for as long as he remains in this ideal and compensatory fantasy, Midas is quite unconscious of the fact that he suffers at all. His life is blinkered and shackled, but so long as he looks straight ahead and takes little steps he doesn't notice and none of it seems to matter.

In our hearts we know that all his efforts are bound to end in tragedy, but if practised sufficiently, they may never have to be experienced as such. For the innocent there are no tragedies. Tragedy is for others. For as long as Midas consistently preserves the fantasy of his unravished innocence, tragedy will never touch him. He need take no responsibilities, no risks, need not run the painful possibility of failure nor the anxieties of separation. Moreover he need have no truck with moral dilemmas, for, as long as he's innocent, there are no rules to abide by because rules and morality only apply to those who have lost their innocence.

Midas need never take anyone else into consideration because his innocence means he's incapable of harming or hurting. There is no need for constraint or limitation to his actions, all of which means that Midas is permanently and dangerously in touch with the transcendent realms to whom the shackles of mortal responsibility are but a vaguely nagging irritation. The potential for tyranny and for repeating the patterns of his destructive childhood against both himself and others begin to emerge.

One of the 'delights' of Hyperborea is that it is a land of 'eternal harmony'. It is, however, also a land of 'prohibitive harmony' (Zorn, ibid) that brooks no friction or discord. This means that one can have no independent judgements, no personal reference points or individual tastes since this might clash with the judgements, tastes or preferences of others. That would not be harmonious. The true self that dares to take a stand must be expunged and cast out for the sake of this 'harmony'. Authentic reality must be crushed underfoot.

Without this possibility for contrast or comparison, there can be no values, no way of measuring what is significant or of distinguishing good evil or right from wrong. A fog of unreality in which his self-destructiveness is given leave to conceal itself rises from the earth infecting the air of his kingdom with a pall of hypocrisy and cowardice. Because real life contains situations that are not ideal, real life cannot be entered into. It can only be observed from the side lines with a 'specious glow of false and deceptive contentment' (Zorn, ibid). Stuck on the sidelines and without recourse to his own authority, Midas must surrender his personal will and exercise his power without discrimination, bringing himself and all he touches inexorably closer to the metaphorical high cliffs upon which he is already blindly teetering when Silenus makes his appearance.

Poetically enough, the name 'Hyperborea' also means 'those who carry around or over'. They don't go through. They sidestep their experience or rise above it like so many of us whose purpose in life is to carry our personae intact around or over the body of our authentic experience, searching for ways to circumvent it as though it were somehow unworthy of our attention. In the process we also circumvent the natural authority of our own judgement and can no longer refer to our inner world as a source of guidance.

Just this evening I interviewed a young woman who wanted to begin a course of psychotherapy. I noticed in the preliminary form that she'd filled out, two references to 'dumping her anger'. I enquired about this. She's furious with her mother for interfering in her relationships, trying to dictate her career, for making her feel guilty. 'And … ?' I ask, feeling that her fury seems quite justifiable. 'Well, I want to dump it, I love her really, the anger gets in the way, it makes our relationship cold.' The winter chill of discontent cannot be borne in Hyperborea. Nor the ambivalent feelings of both love and hate represented by Eusebes and Machimus. She wants 'to get back to the time when everything was fine', to get around or over her anger so that it need not complicate her ideal world.

Her problem was not so much her rage, or even her lack of separation from her mother, but the refusal to go through her authentic experience in order to truly find herself. This, however, would entail her sacrificing at altars other than that of Apollo, the sole God of Hyperborea. Not that there's anything wrong with Apollo. Life would be intolerable without a God of Light and healing. It's just that when he is the only God to whom credit is given he gets a bit out of balance. His often caustic and instructive healing becomes a mere palliative of 'making it better', and lacks the deep panacea we get when Apollo works in conjunction with his dark brother Dionysus who recognises the healing inherent in accepting life's burdens. Without the load of life's burden we lose our footing on the ground of real human experience. Deprived of the gravity of authentic realities, such as the anger reported by the woman above, we remain floating off in a land of fantasy and compensatory idealisations where the paradoxes of the real world cannot be contained, nor any real growth sustained.

The fact that Midas' idealisations exist in this unholy wedlock with his destructive behaviour is not so hard to see. We need only look as far as western culture to verify the truth of this. We believe that ours is the ideal society, the pinnacle of civilisation, and have exported our ideals throughout the world, forcing them on others if necessary, in the name of 'democracy' and 'progress'. The great diversity and richness of the planet's varied cultures, like the richness and diversity of the authentic self, have been destroyed in the perpetuity of the ideal. Genocides, like that of the Aborigines, the Jews and the American Indians, empire building such as that typified by the 'scramble for Africa' at the end of the last century, and, latterly, the exploitation of the natural world have given rise to mass destruction of the environment. All have their roots and their justifications in ideals that are as grounded in reality as Midas' wish to turn things to gold.

Our visions of ourselves as innocents mean that we have been given leave to destroy with impunity. Conscience is all too horribly cleared of guilt or shame because it was all done in the name of an ideal. Our ideals of technological advancement, free enterprise and economic growth are as euphemistic for greed as Midas calling Cybele 'spirited'. They are precisely the veils of collective illusion that permit us to pollute our world to the point where we stand poised upon the high cliffs alongside our mythic colleague Midas, equally oblivious to the dire straits our fine ideals have brought us.

This severance from the realities of our inner world that is necessitated by our idealisations and the deification of self-image, is mirrored and finds its global expression in our severance from nature. We are compelled to destroy nature in order to maintain the illusion of our separateness from it, our superiority over it, and the pontifical precedence of our personal needs over those of the collective whole. This severance nurtures our denial of death and maintains the fantasy that we are somehow nature. Nature, after all, rots.

With reference points in any deeper reality than our rosy self-images we can only set our compasses by the golden calf of our idealised and ungrounded fantasies which rarely have any bearing on the soul's realities and so it should come as no surprise that we find ourselves driven onto the rocks of a thoroughly self-destructive neurosis. Most of us, however, remain undeterred. We believe that the psyche is what we know of it and, like Midas who believes that Gordius is just and wise and that Cybele is the ideal mother, we take our comfortable and compensatory illusions for fact.

The result is that much of life then becomes about the perfection of our ideal images. We ask not who we are but how we appear. Our focus is not on our experience but on how others experience us. We spend the majority of our waking moments anxiously preoccupied with the impression we create on others and on what kind of image we are projecting. Like the Hyperboreans we cease to live life and become onlookers of life. We turn ourselves into objects or commodities to be judged and appraised and do the same to others in turn, perpetuating the depersonalisation and humiliation that our fantasy-self was itself designed to obscure.

The tragedy of all this is not only that the ideal image of ourselves we are eternally pursuing depersonalises us and recreates the very experience we are hoping to escape, but that it cannot and must not be achieved. Once I have attained my ideal, then what? If meaning and purpose are to be derived from pursuing this image of myself what reasons for living remain once this ideal has been attained, especially if the fantasy, like Midas' gold-making, fails to fulfil as it invariably must?

Moreover, all the inner fragments of soul that are incompatible with the idea of ourselves and which have been so effectively put to flight, come home to roost once the chase is over. So, what the attainment or collapse of our ideals actually provides us, is a prodigal neurosis coupled with a deep sense of having been cheated by the values we imagined would sustain us. In the meantime the ideal vision of what we ought to be able to achieve or perform, is so dismissive of what is humanly possible that the creative impulse is stifled before it finds its voice.

Graham has grown up being told 'you can do anything'. It pleased his Cybelian Mother to see her son in this heroic light. The child is faced with a choice between rebelling against these idealistic expectations or subscribing to them. The implicit demand to prop up mother's grandiose world means he must play along. He begins to believe the family myth about his capacities, to see this ideal vision of himself as a virtue rather than as an unrealistic and abusive imposition.

In later life Graham is smitten by a depression that makes him incapable of any creative impulse because his expectations of himself are so high that nothing but perfection will do. He lived under such pressure to perform that performance became impossible, and develops such a sneering attitude towards his ordinariness that ordinary life can not be entered into. Caught between his unattainable vision and the humanity he so despises, life grinds to a standstill, a fate which must come to those who choose to live in a mythic realm where seasons are ever the same.

The Hyperboreans and their contemporary companions are thus condemned to live a provisional life. Their ideals must not be realised and yet the promise of the ideal cannot be renounced. Life is to be lived in pursuit of a goal that must never be won. The vagaries of ordinary life, out of which at least some meaning may be drawn, are dismissed as temporary fillers on the way to something else, the 'real thing' that will happen along shortly. In the meanwhile, life is experienced as a source of eternal frustration, boredom and marking time.

The sad truth is that the Hyperborean spirit doesn't want to be conscious despite all this waiting around for the 'real thing'. Hence Midas' careful avoidance of wishing for anything that might raise his awareness or truly give him something of value. We forget that the real thing, individuation, is synonymous with the Fall, with a sense of being cast out, of not belonging, of taking the lonesome night sea journey. We forget that self-knowledge is an act 'contra naturam', a sin against collective opinion that is punishable by exile and shaming. We prefer to stay in the Garden of Eden with its Hyperborean promises, its associations of innocence, protection by the Almighty and of a life unspoilt by the painful knowledge of good and evil.

We, like Midas, don't want to live with the complexities of conflict and inner contradiction that constitute the human condition which both loves and hates in the same breath, which prays to Gods it doesn't believe in and destroys that which it loves most.

Despite the angel with his flaming sword who stands at the gates of Eden visiting self-destructive neuroses upon all those who try to sneak back into the garden, this does not stop the vast majority of us from trying. In the process we lose sight of our limitations and the discrimination that self-knowledge provides and do as we please out of the vain belief that because we are 'innocents', on the right side of the garden fence, we are incapable of irrevocable destruction. The fact that we are trespassers there is ignored.

Silenus' prophecies, like the apple of Eden, feel intrusive and indigestible to Midas because they reveal things to him that are inconsistent with his circumscribed view of life. He doesn't want to hear that his idealistic perspective on his family life or his corresponding vision of himself is full of unreal distortions and so, like Perceval from the Grail legends, he fails to ask the right question. 'What do you mean, who are the Hyperboreans and what do they have to do with me?'

Midas dismisses Silenus much as we dismiss the glimpses of his passing in our own lives, the repeating dream, the meaningful coincidence, the slip of the tongue, the emotional outburst, or perhaps a series of relationships that all seem to end the same way. We dismiss these nagging shards of the psyche that snap at our heels because taking them seriously would entail a reappraisal of ourselves that threatens the uncomplicated and comfortable ideals we subscribe to, ideals that are expressly if implicitly designed to ward off becoming too conscious of that which we continue to perpetrate against ourselves.

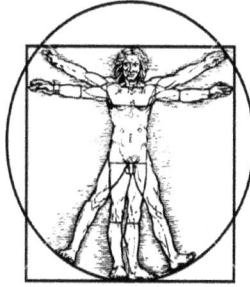

6
Fear, Anxiety and Self-Betrayal

The only thing that makes life possible is permanent, intolerable uncertainty.
Ursula LeGuin

If a hermit crab stays too long in his shell he begins to outgrow it. The shell begins to pinch, forcing him out into the vulnerable open sea-bed without any protection for his bare behind until he can find a more appropriate home, a new and more expansive shell that may or may not provide him with sufficient protection from his vague and half-imagined fears. Such a journey is anxiety-provoking. It's easier to stay in the painfully small shell and suffer its constriction than it is to hazard the unknown.

The anxiety of this vulnerable state is not neurotic. It is the anxiety of facing a prospect that is peopled with fearful expectations. It is difficult to live with but if he fails to face it he sabotages his own evolution and has to shoulder not only his inadequate shell but also a growing sense of self-betrayal. By staying with the familiar, he is compelled to feel the pinch of an identity he has essentially outgrown and the pang of conscience inherent in refusing life's opportunities.

Like the crab, Midas, betrays the push from within. His life remains unlived. The potential to become who he is meant to be must be left untapped. The pain of his childhood can never be realised or released and he is compelled to recreate the familiar destructive patterns of invasion and abandonment that keeps his own backside firmly glued to the shell that he's known for so long.

"In this betrayal [says author and psychotherapist, Piero Ferrucci] ... lies all human pain and human pathology ... we forget ourselves because there is too much change, too much responsibility, too much effort, too much risk maybe. When that happens we create a monster ... the Self is not just going to sit there and let us get away with [our betrayal]. The Self has a will, it wants to incarnate, it has an agenda, it has power and wants to exist in this life. If we deny that, there is going to be a clash and whatever comes out of that clash is going to be

distorted and painful." (1991)

To claim our freedom, to become ourselves, is to stand naked and alone in the face of the sea-bed's dangers with its attendant anxieties. The deconstruction of Midas' idealisations about himself and his past are likewise deeply anxiety provoking. His sense of self depends upon them. To become more fully himself entails a departure from the constricting but familiar experience of things-as-he-knows-them, into a more expansive but thoroughly unknown world that fills him with unfathomed fears.

Midas' self-destructive behaviour is a defence against these inhospitable psychic realities and the anxiety that follows in their wake. It enables him to escape the feelings of loneliness, powerlessness and self-betrayal that his idealisations have cost him. It helps him to get rid of the 'burden of freedom' (Fromm, 1942), the depressing weight of responsibility to his true self and the sense of guilt he has in avoiding this responsibility.

This guilt, like the anxiety of the hermit crab, is authentic and appropriate. It is something for Midas to address in himself and not for him to 'resolve'. It is not neurotic. It is quite different in character to the guilt Midas bears for not being a 'good enough' son. It arises out of the unlived life, his choice to follow the route of least resistance and his refusal to shoulder the burden of freedom. The grief and loss at realising how much of life has been wasted and the self-recrimination for years of refusing to be himself seems too great a load to bear. So he pushes it away, and for the want of his contrition he punishes himself with fresh rounds of destruction.

Paul has been in the country for ten years marking time in an unfulfilling job that 'ties him down'. Finally his residency permit comes through. He has the freedom he's been looking forward to for so long and the prospect of meaningful work that goes with it. But he can hardly get out of bed, spending his patiently awaited freedom on hashish binges that anaesthetise him. I ask what's being anaesthetised. 'It's fear. I've run out of excuses now, but I still can't do anything. I've been tying myself down all this time. I've been wasting my life.'

Paul's 'waiting for his freedom' had been an elaborate hoax to keep alive the ideal fantasy about himself that he 'really wanted to succeed and get on in the world', that he was not afraid, that he was big and strong. This meant so deadening the deeper experience of feeling weak, anxious and afraid that in order to feel anything at all over the threshold of numbness he must stimulate himself to excess with psychedelics, all night parties and anonymous orgies. These in turn begin to constitute the 'wasting of his life' for which further bouts of revelry are required to keep it all from consciousness. Round and round. The healing for this modern Midas is to learn to bear not just his suffering but his real guilt for failing to be himself and the fear of the unknown that underpins such a failure.

The child of Gordius and Cybele is particularly prone to such fears. His ego strength has been so drained in his efforts to comply with their inauthentic scenarios and unwritten rules that new situations with their added pressure and complications are overwhelming. He's like a cat with eight lives gone, cautious and fearful, a wounded brave paddling his broken canoe into a storm. He copes with it all by deriding the world and winds up making himself its victim. He smashes the gifts that life offers saying they're not good enough while secretly he fears to take them up for the demands that life then makes upon him. When he turns his back on life in this way he shuts out the possibility of redeeming himself that new opportunities also contain, and must end up supporting the very cause of his suffering.

When a child is raised in such an atmosphere of overt ambiguity like the one that presides in the Phrygian court, he has to build a world around him of unambiguity, of certainty and security. He has to be able to confirm for himself that he both exists and can survive. The intensity of suffering that self-destruction evokes reassures him that he is in fact alive, a reasonable doubt for a child that's had to tailor and deaden his world sufficiently to make it safe enough to live in.

If a child has not been allowed to bond without being swamped or to separate without being abandoned then he may need visible, tangible and intense proof of his autonomous existence to cut, like Alexander, through the ball of doubt and insecurity that plagues him. 'I hurt, I bleed, therefore I am' (Woods & Woods, 1982). This may seem bizarre from the outside, but from the inside a sense of self is maintained by identifying with the potent feelings that acts of self-destruction evoke. It's a trade-off against the sneaking suspicion and the terrible anxiety that the child is not quite real in its own right, that it does not exist save as a strut in the parents' shaky world.

The unconscious attraction of self-destructive behaviour is its power to preoccupy us and prevent us from descending into this inner pit of anxiety from which we secretly fear we may never emerge. 'If the individual cannot take the realness, aliveness, autonomy and identity of himself and others for granted, then he has to become absorbed in contriving ways of trying to be real to prevent himself losing his self.' (Laing, ibid). Self-destructiveness provides us with such absorption and helps us to feel real, not just because self-destructiveness identifies us with the powerful aggressor or that it affirms that there is a self that's being destroyed, but also because self-destructiveness holds our attention sufficiently to prevent us from slipping into the world of unreality that the child of Gordius and Cybele cannot help but harbour in his heart.

Denise is compulsively involved with a man, an alcoholic gambler, who seems to give her nothing but pain and aggravation. She hates this and wants to leave him. On closer inspection she discovers that he is actually really rather valuable to her. All the external chaos of their relationship preserves her from experiencing her inner chaos which has to take a back seat for as long as he is forefront in her mind. Her preoccupation with him provides an exclusion zone between her and the inner despair that threatens to engulf her. The obsessive fixation on an object or person 'out there' means that there's little left over to pay attention to her subjective condition which is, in fact, one of extreme anxiety and panic. Her compulsion is in fact not 'the problem' at all, but a perverse and provisional solution to an even deeper issue that cannot be named. the chaotic and despairing inner child (of an alcoholic gambler), a child who is only really assured of her existence and reality when she is on the familiar receiving end of another's abuse.

This 'compulsion to inflict new suffering on oneself to keep former suffering repressed' (Miller, 1990) is extremely effective. What better solution to keep one's inner chaos at bay than to plunge oneself into an outer chaos that mirrors it exactly - especially if the illusion of control, 'I could leave him if I wanted to', can be maintained? When outer conditions can be created to mirror inner ones, the inner ones disappear from view. A black cat in a dark room isn't there. Denise shifts the conflict with her father onto this other man so that her idealisation of childhood can remain intact and the reality of the child's inner pit of despair kept safely out of sight.

We forget that the self-destructiveness of such compulsive repetitions serve a profound purpose - to preserve us from unbearable grief and pain. We might pay heavily for it: Denise could not get free of this man to whom she felt so compellingly attached, but she was permitted to continue living with the illusion of parents 'who only wanted the best'. For as long as she went out with men who abused her, her father was only normal, an ordinary man among ordinary men. To run the risk of a good experience would have given her something tangible to measure her father by, a yardstick that could no longer deny the terror and unpredictability, one that could measure his drunken abuse for what it was.

Self-destructiveness is born out of the compulsion to repeat our histories rather than experience them. This repetition gives the painful facts of childhood foliage to hide in. It vindicates the actions of Cybele and Gordius and perpetuates the compensatory fantasy that we grew up in a land of milk and honey.

To live to the full is to experience the reality of our ephemeral nature, of the ultimate lack of protection we have from fate. Self-destructive behaviour and the obsessive compulsive forms it often takes, contain the anxiety inherent to such uncertainty. Compulsive behaviour, like ritual, puts the participant into the timeless state of Hyperborea where his anxiety is momentarily transcended, where there is a sense of having power over that nagging fearfulness of things as they are.

The freedom to approach life without preconceptions is an uneasy liberation. Every step of the way is going to compel Midas to re-examine himself, to live with contradiction and paradox, to hold up for clearer inspection the suspect truths that he's carved in stone to convince himself of their reality. When asked who he is he wants to be able to give an unambiguous answer. Yet beneath it all churns the lurking anxiety, the sneaking suspicion that he is not quite real. Not only is he at sea but he's also thrown the instruments of navigation into the water so as not to measure the extent of his dereliction.

Life is scary. The Universe constantly confronts us with the unknown, demanding of us that we manage it in some way even though we have few precedents to fall back on. When a child has been brought up with tolerable fears, then the demands of individuation in adult life will not be overly taxing. But if it has spent much of its life having to bear the burden of Cybele's anxieties and Gordius' depression and had no one to contain his own fears, then the anxieties that many of us consider to be the normal hitches of everyday life soon assume unbearable proportions.

When parents are so preoccupied that they cannot mirror the child's fears back to them in a way that makes them tolerable, then the child is compelled to retreat from life. This retreat entails the active destruction of the impulse to dare and be itself. The child becomes rigid, it cannot let go of having to be in control, or allow the deconstruction of itself that integrating new ideas, fresh concepts or strange experiences require.

When something unknown faces us, it challenges our world view. It's unknown precisely because our way of seeing things cannot accommodate it. In order to do so, we are compelled to realise that our views are narrower than we had thought, that we were wrong, prejudiced, mistaken or ignorant. The whole process of discovering requires of us that we hold our constructs lightly, that we be willing to relinquish outmoded ideas of who we are. This takes considerable courage since our way of seeing things is a source of identity. When we learn things our identity changes. We have to deconstruct ourselves to some extent in order to really assimilate our new life.

This process of deconstruction is scary. Too much deconstruction leads to disintegration, a shattering of identity. When identity is already precarious, then any deconstruction whatsoever becomes a source of great anxiety. It doesn't take much dynamite to bring down a building with cracked foundations. Creative living is not simply a question of adding on new rooms or new stories to the already existing structure, but about 'seeing everything fresh all the time' (Winnicott, 1986). The inner building is in a state of constant but gradual transformation that is stimulating and exciting if one is secure enough within oneself, but a source of great anxiety if the fundamentals of life have been left unattended.

Anne's presenting issue is her low self-esteem. She feels panicky, the need to please is palpable in the room. She criticises and runs herself down continuously. She is intensely self-conscious about her appearance and talks at great length about the quality of her skin. She feels victimised, invaded and describes herself as poisoned. In time she confesses that she also feels frigid and 'has no feeling down there'. The reality is that she has little feeling whatsoever. There is a 'hole in her heart'. She feels empty, and describes her childhood as being one of a china doll on show. One with perfect porcelain skin but ultimately fragile and hollow.

Anne's parents were classically Phrygian. Her Cybelian mother was invasive and hysterical, their relationship was a 'mishmash' based on 'I met my needs by meeting hers'. Anne's father lacked presence to such a degree that it was four years before he was able to become significant in our work together. Her conscious attitude was that she wanted to be more spontaneous, to 'let go', to regain her sexual feeling and find her own spirit which had been so crushed that her spine had become twisted into a scoliosis out of somatic sympathy. The deeper reality was that she was terrified of all these possibilities. Her sense of self was not sufficiently formed to be able to 'let go'.

The prospect of separating out from Mother meant facing her own fragmentation at Mother's hands, the discovery of the full extent to which she had been crushed was attended by explosive feelings that threatened to blow her apart. The prospect of rediscovering her sexuality and unnumbing her body meant feeling its pain and letting go in orgasm that was far too much an experience of being out of control for her fragile sense of self to encompass. Anne's prevailing belief was that she simply wanted to 'be positive' and to move forward. It took a dream to rebalance her conscious attitude. 'I'm in a great building that I know is my body. There is a nerve centre, a computer, that governs my sexuality. Someone is throwing switches to find the right combination. I run away in terror trying desperately to find a way out.'

Anne's problem was not so much that she couldn't feel her sexuality but that she was terrified to do so. Her terror, like her body, had been numbed, and so it had to be for her to hold herself together sufficiently to withstand the onslaught from her mother and the flight of her father. The self-destructive sacrifice of bodily aliveness paled into insignificance next to her need to contain herself and keep her fears at arms length, though it was at one and the same time the price she paid for keeping her life on hold.

Self-destructiveness sets in with a vengeance when life presents us with a challenge which for one reason or another we feel unable to meet. The self-destructive act, whether deliberate or not, buys time in which we secretly hope to find the ego strength to master the challenge and avoid the humiliation of a defeat. This may range from the totally unconscious numbing of the body in which Anne took refuge from her fears of being unable to cope with adult sexual life, to the quite deliberate self-destructiveness of the schoolboy who breaks his finger so that he doesn't have to sit an exam he's afraid he'll fail. In either instance a period of grace is granted from the fear of failure or sense of being overwhelmed that threatens to excessively disrupt the person's world.

Much as we crave our freedom from the shackles of family legacies that hobble our individuation we also fear and avoid it. To be free is to be alone. Gone are the hopes for the magic helper, the imagined rescuer, the ideal parent we craved for that will bind our wounds and carry us, like Virgil, over the ditches of Dante's inferno and past the dread images of life with its comforting illusions stripped away.

> Then my master caught me up like a mother ...
> Carrying me off, hugged close to his breast
> Truly not like a comrade, but a son.
> Above us, there they were! The demons! But he, at large
> In the other chasm, could set his fears at rest.

It is difficult to let such hopes of deliverance die! We keep them alive with little acts of self-destruction that buy time for us while we wait around kicking our heels for the arrival of that special someone who'll cut through Gordius' knot and liberate us from our plight. Unfortunately, because much of our self-destruction is unconscious, we cannot use the time we buy with it to better prepare ourselves for the feared event because the acknowledgement of such a need would require consciousness of the situation we are in – the very source of the fear itself. In other words the purpose of self-destruction can never be made explicit and therefore never used to advantage. It can only ever obscure the real issues sufficiently to lessen their anxiety.

The fact that we are then robbed of our capacity to resolve the source of that anxiety becomes a secondary issue next to the instant gratification of eliminating its symptoms. We remain stuck, impotent and regressed in the process - but at least our vision is circumscribed and blinkered enough to ignore the fact that this is the case. Like an ostrich with its head in the sand the self-destructive character alleviates himself of the anxiety that a lion may be about, but deprives himself of being able to do something about it. The alleviation of his anxiety actually increases the likelihood of becoming that day's dinner. Seeing no evil isn't a defence against evil, indeed, it makes one more the prey to it.

Midas' self-destructive wish to turn things into gold is an attempt to preserve the ego from the fear of encountering his own undiscovered self. 'The experience of the self', says Jung, 'is always a blow to the ego.' Midas prevents this by ensuring that his wish keeps him firmly in the rut of that which is familiar. He perpetuates his mother's unconscious fantasy of him that he has heroic magical prowess and aligns himself with his father's scorn when it all goes badly wrong. He uses his wish as an opportunity to avoid the individuation that he so secretly fears with all its unfathomed consequences and keeps himself locked in the prison of his own ivory-towered grandiosity.

Midas fears seeing his relationships with his parents for what they are, but he fears even more the deconstruction of his personality with which his freedom from them threatens him. The devil that you know is safer than the angel you do not. The prospect of detoxifying himself from their malign influence throws open the door on a world of myriad possibilities that are overwhelming in their infinite variety. He may have spent much of his life covertly cursing the prison that his family life had built around him, but when faced with his freedom he slams the door on it and retreats into his cell. The experience of imprisonment can never be fully gauged until one has an experience of liberation to compare it with. At least part of the fear of freedom is the horror of having the means by which to measure the extent of life's constriction, not to mention the loss of containment that even prison provides.

A client, Billy, learned this in a most graphic way. He had been complaining of his stuckness. I asked how it served him to be so stuck. He took great umbrage at this, redoubling his blaming of circumstance and fate. During the following week he had this dream. 'I am in a jail. I have a baseball bat in my hands and smash it wildly against the bars, screaming to be let out. I hear a soft noise behind me and turn to look. Another man, my cell-mate, is draped lazily over a bunk. He indicates the door casually and says softly, "It's open, you know." I drop the bat and throw myself away from the door in horror.' The gift of such an explicit dream helped him to place in context his own self-destructive behaviour, after all - as the hero/villain of Stephen King's *Cape Fear (1987)* puts it, ' … there's nothing to do in prison but desecrate your flesh.'

Such desecration may feel a little crazy, but at least it is I who am doing it and not the awful fate that desecrates without warning and with unknown strength. In the trap that Midas has created for himself at least he knows what's what. He preserves a sense of identity -

debilitated and crushed though it may be. He has sacrificed his freedom for the maintenance of things-as-he-knows-them and in so doing avoids the horrible prospect of an even greater madness overtaking him when he stands naked and alone in the face of a future that he suddenly realises he cannot control. If I am not my mother's hero/son with special powers or my father's failure, who am I? If I stop holding the family together what will happen? If I step into the darkness of my own undiscovered self what will I find there? What horrors await me? Even positive circumstances that are alien to the person who has not been given the grace to find his own way will fill the fragmented sense of self with fear.

I'm put in mind of a class I taught recently in which we played through some brief therapy sessions for the purposes of practical learning. The would-be client was complaining at length of how no one supported her, no one listened or gave her any help. It was always she that took care of others.

So far so good, but she said all this in a voice that was almost impossible to hear. The student counsellor had to lean right forward, had to ask her to speak up several times and spent much of the time, quite justifiably, trying to clarify what was being said. Eventually the client blew up, 'You're just like everyone else. You don't listen, you don't support me!'

It was true that few people really listened to her, and yet the only thing that disturbed her more than not being listened to was precisely the awful prospect of really being heard, of actually getting her needs met. She had to sabotage the student counsellor's quite remarkable listening to preserve intact the fragile identity of 'I'm someone no one listens to.' To be truly heard would wash away this identity, not to mention it giving her a means by which to gauge the full extent to which she had been left to her own devices in her life. Her 'not being heard' and the experience of being a victim had to be perpetuated if she was to preserve intact her world view and the vision she had of her place within it.

If we are to grow and change we need to be able to tolerate a certain amount of unreality and not knowing. An old teacher of mine expressed it this way, 'The first time you call yourself a psychotherapist you're a liar. The second time you're a cheat. The third time there may be some truth in it.' This experience of being a cheat is necessary to becoming oneself. The first time we try on a new hat we inevitably feel like a fraud. It takes time for the sense of unreality to wear off, for the hat to become 'ours' and not just something perched on the head. If the transition, with its concomitant feelings of unreality, overly threatens the integrity of the personality, then growth and becoming must be sabotaged for the sake of stability. The hat will be abandoned in some corner.

Kay suffers from a string of mysterious illnesses. A stomach bug she caught on holiday lays her low for six months. The organic cause of the illness clears up in a matter of days but the symptoms persist despite the recovery. She suffers a week or two of good health before succumbing to a series of infections that seem to have no medically diagnosable roots. These are followed by bouts of headaches that keep her in bed for days at a time. She looks increasingly pale. Her demeanour is ever more fey and her voice develops a pleading quality to it. It turns out that just before she went away on her holiday she was given a highly responsible post at work as well as starting up a dance class in her free time. Her low esteem has convinced her that she is incapable of either task. She is dogged by a fear of failure and the feeling that she is a fraud. The conviction of others that she is an effective manager and an adequate teacher fills her with unreality when it collides with her deeply held conviction that she is no good. There is no recourse but to retreat into illness. This gives her a way of accounting for her 'poor performance' and mediates the feeling of unreality that a transition into more effective living and successfully becoming herself engenders. Her feelings of being a fraud are not neurotic. It is the retreat from unreality that is the problem and not the unreality itself.

We assume that all unreality is pathological, something to be 'fixed'. Very often, the experiences of unreality are simply the heralds of the potential self announcing its unexpected arrival. The personality experiences this like the disruptive gatecrashing of an uninvited guest at a carefully orchestrated party and evicts it before enquiring what gifts it bears. Fairy tales like 'Sleeping Beauty' and 'The Glass Coffin', in which the ego pays for their eviction by falling into a coma, show quite clearly what happens when the uninvited guest is driven out. Boredom, neglect, illness and a kind of living death begin to set in, sapping the personality of its zest and vitality. For Kay, the refusal to embody the authentic feelings of being a fraud meant that she condemned herself to a neurotic retreat from life.

We need to distinguish the healthy unreality and disorientation weathered in the transition from one shore of our soul to another, from the neurotic unreality of refusing to make the very crossing that outer circumstance and inner impetus demand. We cannot escape the experience of unreality. The only choice is whether we experience it within the context of a meaningful transition into world unknown, or as a consequence of the life unlived where we are the powerless victims of the rejected self, that uninvited guest who forces us, with disastrous consequences, to lie in the beds we have made for ourselves.

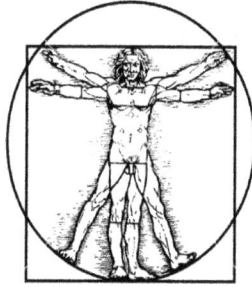

7
Attachment to Suffering

Not so swiftly does a man renounce that which has entered his
blood stream, that which he has ...received in his mother's milk.
Dostoevsky: The House of the Dead

Midas is unable to face his fears and take that step into the unknown of his authentic inner world. In the process he is compelled to repeat the history he will not let himself experience. Enacted suffering of this sort is far preferable to the fragile personality than suffering that comes from within. Midas can play victim and account for the experience of being 'done to' by pointing to the blows of fate that rain down upon him. His idealised childhood remains intact, while his feelings of outrage can be safely generalised or displaced to a more manageable situation.

Let's take an example. Rachel's presenting issue is that she is unable to trust her husband with other women despite his giving no direct cause for her concern. The roots of this seem to be in her relationship with her father who sexually abused her over a ten-year period. She had no one to go to for support (her mother was in a mental hospital for manic depression for much of the time) and so she rationalised away her feelings, 'Well, he was a horny man and naturally went for us young girls. He had a tough time with Ma, poor guy.'

Such justification may well have saved her from unbearable suffering as a child, but it was now crippling her adulthood. The feeling of betrayal and abandonment that she could not allow to be part of her childhood experience now permeated her adult life where she was being compelled to suffer it all over again without any hope of resolution since her husband's fidelity was in fact not the issue.

The preservation of the image of her ideal father necessitated a generalisation of his behaviour to all 'horny young men', who 'naturally' have sex with anyone to hand. How could she possibly trust her husband in the face of such a belief system? She could not. Nor could she leave him for that would constitute the beginning of a protest against the arbitrary rampancy of 'horny young men'. She had to stay with her husband and continue to suffer her paranoia.

Indeed, she was deeply attached to her suffering since it afforded her the comfortable fantasy of her father's love despite his abuse. After all, 'boys will be boys'.

The authentic experience of suffering is most effectively defended against by throwing oneself into fresh suffering, a substitute preoccupation for the fragile ego upon whom the reality of unbearable pain threatens to descend at the first unguarded moment. The person must surround himself with suffering, must attract pain and compel himself into situations which are adverse or detrimental so that the particular sufferings of that unique and individual life are enfolded, disguised and consumed in the embrace of something far more impersonal.

The consistent hammering with which life then obliges us can then be seen as something inherent to living itself and not just to my life. This draws the sting from the experience of evil or malevolence that has been personally meted out against us, and allows us to live out our illusions as well as our self-destructiveness with some measure of good conscience.

Anne has 'once more been let down by men'. Her latest boyfriend is 'like all the others, not there for me, not able to commit or really be involved'. Anne explains this to herself by attributing this absent quality to men in general as Rachel did with her father's sexuality. The deeper reality is that Anne's father was classically Gordian – absent, demanding, perfectionistic. In order to preserve herself from the pain of the implicit rejection inherent in his inability to relate to her, she blames and demands perfection of herself, 'If only I were more X or Y or Z then he'd be there for me.' This keeps her hope for nurture alive.

In the meantime Anne must avoid being really nurtured like the plague. She must unconsciously go for men who are like her father so that her father's failure and the real extent of his limitations not be shown up for what they are. She must cling to her empty relationships and the suffering of life without intimacy if she is to maintain the distant hope that one day her father will meet her needs and be with her in the way she so desperately needs. In the meantime she drives herself into the ground trying to be more acceptable to him out of the vain assumption that his frozenness is somehow a response to her insufficiency rather than it simply being an immutable expression of who he is, a state of being that she is in fact impotent to affect or change.

For as long as we are convinced of our sin, under the delusion that such approbation will secure the life-giving nurture that the Phrygian child so deeply needs, we must invite suffering upon ourselves in endless acts of unconscious contrition. Attachment to suffering obscures painful truths and keeps hope alive. A self-destructive neurosis is traded off against unbearable realities we fear will destroy us.

Sam describes himself as desperate for love. More than anything he craves the attention and nurture he never received as a child, but he cannot accept it when it is offered to him. When his girlfriend says she loves him or praises him he shrugs it off and likewise when he misses a session with me he believes I'm going to punish him and throw him out for 'not being committed', despite the long and warm relationship we've enjoyed. He craves love but cannot let it in. He clings onto the pain of his loveless world. I place an object on the couch next to him, something to embody good things. I invite him to help himself and to notice what happens as he contemplates meeting his own needs and accepting what's available. He shrinks back. 'I can't. I feel like a thief.'

There lay the nub of Sam's difficulty. Despite his rage at inadequate and paranoid parents there existed a deep identification with them that still saw the child in him as culpable of the crime of wanting love. The overwhelming feeling of guilt that he associated with getting his needs met could not be borne, let alone the resentment that under-pinned it. He had to remain firmly attached to his loveless suffering and emptiness even when love was made available to him so that his healthy rage and the real feelings of loss and deprivation could be kept from the cold light of day. The prospect of letting love in brought to the surface the feeling of being a thief, the sense of lack that makes a person steal in the first place, as well as the glaring comparisons he could begin to make of his early life once in possession of this strange and novel feeling of warmth and fullness.

This attachment to suffering then begins to create a vicious circle. The real life of the person gets deadened by the repression and avoidance of good things. The thwarted desire to love and be loved creates a sterile desert of depression and heaviness in the person that can only be cut through momentarily by further acts of self-destruction. Life has become so boring and drab that only the intense adrenalin evoked by repeated blows to the system can shock the person into some semblance of living.

The person now begins to require the drama of destructiveness to rouse himself out of his enervated mire. This, like any shot in the arm, works for a while, but in the long term it only contributes to the very experience of being half alive that the self-destructive behaviour was unconsciously intended to counter. The solution aggravates the problem and the only way out is for the person to experience the despair of their Catch-22 situation and allow the depression that follows to run its course.

The experience of suffering throughout life can be so consistent, that it becomes identified with one's very being. Suffering becomes a way of knowing oneself and to be deprived of this suffering then constitutes a source of acute anxiety. While working in a residential home for ex-mental patients, I once made the foolish error of trying to deprive one of the residents of her diagnostic label. In my naivety, I assumed that being called 'schizophrenic' was at best mildly insulting and at worst a damnation of the soul. I perceived her liberal use of these labels as a way putting herself down and felt the heroic compulsion to encourage her to view her problems in a more 'positive' light. She hit the roof. 'I am schizophrenic! I am schizophrenic!' she screamed, pounding the arms of her chair with both fists.

Implicit in her explosion was the sentiment, 'How dare you deprive me of the only way I have of knowing myself', the only thing of which I am sure any more? Let me at least have this one stable thing in my crazy life.' In lesser ways the rest of us turn a blind eye to the possibilities for our own peace of mind and covertly keep the wheels of our neurosis turning.

Consistent suffering has a happy way of becoming 'normal', almost unnoticeable by virtue of its day-to-dayness. More than this it gives us a sense of identity, enough for us to make sure that we have our 'agony on hand' because it gives the person 'the right to be who he is' (Kierkegaard, 1949). To be deprived of this 'right' makes it conspicuous by its absence. What had been a familiarly undefined and vaguely furry presence in the shadows of the psyche is now illumined and thrown into sharp contrast by the experience of something quite different. This we cannot allow and so we must repress the sublime and avoid life's beneficence lest it bring into focus that greater portion of life that has been lived in the dark. Perhaps this is the thought behind the proverb, 'don't ask too loudly for what you want, you might just get it'.

Persian folklore tells a story that epitomises this ambivalence. A man had spent his whole life looking for God. He had searched everywhere, high and low, near and far. Despite his unsuccessful efforts he never gave up his searching and though he had now become old and wizened he persisted with his life-long attempt to find him. One day he was pursuing his search and came across a sign that said 'God', and pointed him in the direction. He went cautiously down the path until he came to a house with a notice outside that said, 'God lives here', whereupon he quietly removed his shoes and tiptoed away.

If our suffering has become a source of identity, the opportunity for some relief is bound to be met with mixed feelings. When the ego has been weakened by the unnumbered invasions and dismissals of significant others and has learnt that to live is to be crushed, then all its forces have to be mustered in the maintenance of the half-alive self it has been compelled to become. This is not just to remain congruent with parental powers but also because the ego has become so fragile that the contradiction of what it knows cannot be tolerated.

The real being of the child soon becomes so lost in the maintenance of life's lie, that authentic memories and experiences that advocate the unfolding of the true self may well feel like persecutory attacks that must be defended against at all costs. The ego, 'mistaking the real for the false self' (Winnicott, 1986) experiences the potential collapse of the false self as life threatening and so with ultimate irony, 'the ego will marshal all defences even to the point of destroying the life of the real human being' (Johnson, 1987).

Sid had obviously been in some kind of therapy before. He launched in from the word go, a tirade of condemnation against his father, using buzz words like 'intrusion' and 'inner child', how hurt and wounded he was, how abusive his childhood had been, what opportunities he had been deprived of. Yet something in me just could not respond to this man. I felt utterly flat. My compassion lay like a fat dog in front of a hot fire, and barely cocked an ear at this melancholy outpouring of misery and dejection.

For several weeks he harangued me with tales of woe designed to squeeze pity out of me, but it was like trying to get blood from a stone. I began to wonder if I was seriously in danger of losing my capacity to empathise with my clients. Maybe I was in the wrong job. Perhaps I was getting cynical. Then one day Sid began the tale of how his father had first beaten him. The old dog in me rolled over but still stayed sound asleep. His father had been warning him not to sprinkle him with a hose pipe, some game that Sid had pushed too far in the back garden. Sid squirted him again and his Dad said 'If you touch that pipe again I'll beat you.' Sid put the pipe down, let it sit a moment then picked it up 'to put it away'. He had touched the hose pipe and received the promised thrashing. How unfair! how cruel! 'I was only putting it away, but no, he's so rigid, he knew that's all I was doing but he had to fulfil the letter of the law.'

Ah, but now the game was up. 'Sid, you knew that was going to happen, didn't you?' The question hung in the air like a lead balloon. 'Well, …I suppose.' He confessed sheepishly. 'So what's it all about?' I asked. Sid shrugged 'My sense,' I began, 'is that you gained some kind of victory over him. What happens if you fail to evoke your father's persecution?' 'Well, I couldn't go to Mother and join her sneering at him', replied Sid with dawning comprehension. 'And if you and Mother don't sneer at Father and the world, what then?' 'Well,' said Sid haltingly, 'I don't really exist.'

The old dog by his fireside woke up with a start as Sid began to speak softly about the collusive relationship with his mother, how between them they kept his father outside their cordoned-off sanctuary, isolated and ridiculed him, how Sid carried her passive hatred of his father in return for this feeling of specialness and how her love seemed to depend on the sense of being better than him and everyone else. To keep her, and the sense of aliveness she promised, Sid was compelled into a life of victimhood and suffering, suffering that paradoxically meant safety and the long lost promise of Mama's life-giving, if conditional affection.

Most of us go into therapy hoping to be relieved of our suffering. Little do we suspect our attachment to suffering or the sense of identity it provides. Our romantic fantasy that all we wish for is to grow and change is precisely what prevents us from becoming ourselves. Our pride will not countenance the possibility that we cling to our suffering like the drowning clutch at straws nor that our suffering is something we invest in. Actually transforming our self-destructiveness often means relinquishing world views in which we have unconsciously cast ourselves as the victim.

To change is to raise the gnawing question - 'if I do not suffer or am not in pain who am I?' This is very threatening. It means the end of something that much of our being takes as immutable fact, let alone the threat of abandonment or annihilation that goes with it. The shudder that permeates what we imagined to be immovable is profoundly unsettling. Such changes also bring to mind the fact that everything ultimately ends, and in the wings of life's play is awareness of the final curtain. Our death anxiety is something we make a life project of keeping at arm's length, primarily by preventing change, especially the change of hallowed and primordial truths about ourselves or the world that we were fed along with mother's milk. We can live with an illusion of immanent eternity for as long as things are kept the same. Life might be a nightmare in the process, but at least it is a stable nightmare and a dream of something.

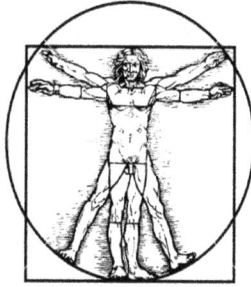

8
Madness and Ecstasy

Our only health is the disease
If we obey the dying nurse
Whose constant care is not to please
But to remind of our and Adam's curse
And that to be restored our sickness must grow worse.
T.S. Eliot

Midas' encounter with Silenus is a missed opportunity for psychological development. He's unwilling or unable to fathom the truth about himself that Silenus has to offer. His ego structures are still too one-sided and rigid, or too fragile to include the disturbing richness of paradox and feeling that constitutes the complexities of the true self. Something else has to happen before the people of Eusebes and Machimus can feel at home on earth, and Silenus has to refer Midas to a practitioner with different methods of awakening consciousness.

Midas returns to Dionysus' camp with Silenus amidst great pomp and ceremony. Having learnt nothing from his instruction he is now simply fulfilling his kingly duties. His naive conception of the world, necessitated by the repression of his own authority and natural intelligence, means he's unable to see that this Demigod Silenus is actually leading him to the Dionysian camp for a second, hopefully more successful initiation, into a deeper more authentic experience of himself.

Dionysus plays along. He thanks Midas for 'returning' Silenus and grants him a wish out of 'gratitude', knowing full well that Midas will ask for something that takes to the limit his naive and compensatory world view, something that will serve to further suppress and gag the voice of his stifling soul from telling its truth. Predictably, Midas asks for his narrow and increasingly shallow self-image to be consolidated by being able to turn everything he touches into gold. Perhaps he hopes that this external fascination will suffice to silence once and for all the distant yet audible struggling of his inner world.

Dionysus grants the wish after making absolutely sure that this is exactly what Midas wants. He knows that Midas is about to incur upon himself a full-blown bout of self-destruction. Once he's sure that the king is going into this experience with his eyes open, he gives him what he's asked for in the hope that this will be sufficient to generate the self-reflection required to out grow the gilded cage that Midas is creating for himself.

Dionysus knows that no amount of lecturing is going to evoke insight from Midas. But he also knows that granting Midas his wish is going to backfire on him, and that pretty soon the reality of what is really going on will burst through the mask of the false self and confront Midas with the reality of that from which he has hidden for so long.

The only way to remain unconscious of our self-betrayal is to continue to betray ourselves. Neuroses have to escalate if they are to be maintained. Their subtle and easily rationalised beginnings must sooner or later blow their cover as things become ever more apparent, even to the averted eye. The repression of the true self contains the seeds of its own undoings even if it takes a thoroughgoing neurosis to rub our noses in the fact that something is seriously amiss. It might take a series of panic attacks to draw attention to the bland and emotionally crippled life that this explosion of feelings compensates. It might take a tyrannical lover to remind us, by association, of a mother we'd prefer to remember as sweet and cuddly. It might take a heart-attack to remind us that we have a heart.

For a while, the fulfilment of Midas' wish brings him some amusement. First he picks up a twig. It instantly turns to gold and he shouts with delight. Then he picks up a stone. It is at once a nugget of pure gold. Midas is overjoyed. He calls for his daughter the princess to share the great news and embraces her, realising too late that his kiss is as deadly to her as a stab to the heart. She becomes a gold statue, cold and lifeless. Midas' shock is as sudden as his joy was moments earlier and it's through this shock that the reality of what he has asked for slowly sinks in. He orders food to be brought to console and divert him, but when that too is turned to gold the truth of his situation dawns in all its ugliness and the despair that his glittering wish was designed to keep at bay comes flooding in.

Our attitude towards neuroses is perverted by the prejudice that they are lacking in instruction. Craziness only looks like nonsense or mere chaos when viewed out of context. Because we don't understand it we assume it cannot be understood. By definition we call anything that falls outside our own reference points as crazy or at least ridiculous, and yet nothing could be further from the truth. Neurosis is the language of the soul in exile. If we dig just a little beneath the surface and take into consideration the unpleasant realities that Midas is so desperate to keep concealed from himself we might begin to appreciate the poetic skill with which his wish begins to wake him up.

The soul will communicate itself to us in whatever way it has to or is forced to. Its messengers will arrive at our doorstep battered, bruised and bloodied having run the gauntlet of the ego's defences, but arrive they will – late, exhausted and mildly incoherent after their exertions, but, like the mounties, they always get their man. Our task is to listen between their gasps for breath, and to make what we can of their message.

Midas' final hurdle to the unequivocal confrontation with his true self is his protestation to Dionysus and his begging to have everything returned back to normal, back to his neurotic adaptation and false complacency. These protests are the last line of defence against the full horror of his self-destruction and the reality of his despairing inner world. We could compare his remonstrations with Faust's complaint against Mephistopheles in Goethe's epic. Faust wished for youth after the same fashion that Midas wished for gold. He was none too pleased with the result either, and chided Mephistopheles who in turn reminded him that his wish was not for contentment or happiness but for youth, with all its ups and downs. The dark god has an annoying habit of following our requests to the letter and we can imagine Dionysus saying much the same to Midas 'you asked not to be rich or to have much gold, but to turn things to gold and that's what you've got'.

The dark god makes us live with the consequences of our actions precisely to enable us to experience just how restricting are the cages we've built ourselves, just how contrived and inauthentic our false masks. For as long as we call this 'malign' or 'evil', we've failed to learn the lesson and have to face further hells until we do. We protest our innocence in order not to have to acknowledge what we are intuitively beginning to realise is a hollow and superficial, way of life. We protest in order to turn away one more time from the painful fact of our empty pursuit after petty irrelevancies that preoccupy us sufficiently to keep at arm's length the pain, fear and horror of our self-destructiveness. We do it in order not to feel the weight of responsibility and guilt for all the waste and loss and damage that we have incurred upon ourselves.

For as long as Midas blames Dionysus with the likes of 'Why me? Why didn't you warn me/ protect me/save me?' he can preserve himself from the sting hidden in the real questions, 'What have I done? Who did I believe myself to be? What does all this say about me and where I've come from? What is it about this despair and isolation that feels so familiar? If this is not what I want, what do I want?' Such questions constitute the barque that ferries us to a more expansive shore of the soul, but the journey itself is an experience of purgatory, a fall from grace.

Ironically enough this may feel to Midas as if he were going mad and yet it is in fact the end of his lifelong sojourn in unreality. Midas' acknowledgement of his compensatory pride, his compulsive greed, his learned use of others as objects and the underlying reality of his alienation from himself is a tremendous blow to the false world he has constructed for his ease and comfort. Though his feigned naivety was a sterile cage, its loss is the loss of his identity and it feels tantamount to being cast out of paradise. The authentic guilt, the genuine shame and the despair are overwhelming.

In his efforts to avoid being in pain, Midas has found himself precisely in pain. The only way out of his neurotic pain is to experience the authentic pain that lies beneath it. In despair, Midas is confronted by the destructive shadow of his compliant facade, the truth of his underlying torment and is forced to realise - by the very means designed to keep it under wraps - that all is not what it seems. This is a great breakthrough for Midas and a moment of crucial importance. He has persisted in his folly and become wise. He has stopped pointing the finger. He stops begging Dionysus to rid him of his symptoms and asks instead how he may atone for his sin against himself. He asks for help. Gone is the blaming, cajoling and demanding. The false and compensatory sense of 'I can do anything' that the wish was designed to fuel has collapsed and the authentic underlying reality of impotence and frustration revealed for what it is, his true feelings. The vulnerability of his authentic reality shows itself for the first time.

This transformation is the altered state for which Dionysus is so justly famed in perpetrating. He is the god of chaos, dismemberment, death and rebirth. Midas must truly have been half asleep to imagine he would escape Dionysus peculiar talents, for he is that archetypal power responsible for initiatory transformations. When Midas stops fighting this process, when he surrenders and admits the hopelessness of his situation the dark god relents and instructs him how to redeem himself by bathing in the source of the river Pactolus.

Dionysus doesn't shame Midas by doing it for him. He simply tells him how to help himself - by acknowledging soul, represented by the spring that is the river's source, as being at the heart of his being. When the false self is acknowledged as such, allowed to die, despair embraced and hope abandoned, then and only then the dark god points the way to redemption and a new beginning.

Dionysus is popularly conceived as a god of drunken revelry and orgiastic rites, and so he was, but we assume too little if we make of this that he was merely a god of excess and indulgence. The raison d'étre of the Dionysian cult in ancient times was ecstasy, the initiation and transformation of the soul through 'enthusiasmos' into a profound alteration of the personality. Ecstasy is the privilege of those who have managed to relocate the source of worth within their own inviolable hearts. Ecstasy is the acceptance and realisation of what one is rather than what one has or does. This is difficult for Midas who believes he's only as good as his capacity to make things happen, his ability to turn things into gold. Midas is necessarily in conflict with that very part of him in which his ecstasy resides. He is set against nature, both his own personal nature and that of the natural world. Hence the excessive self-control and destructive 'harnessing' of nature that characterise our epoch.

We enviously attack the natural child within us so as not to have the hollow sham of the accumulative character shown up for what it is. If our identity rests on what we have amassed, or what we do in life, then the pure being that Dionysus advocates threatens our entire way of knowing ourselves. We cast him in the role of the devil and combat our bliss with all the ferocity of a life and death struggle. The extensiveness of this struggle can be seen mirrored in the genocides of primitive peoples who are ambassadors of the world of being, who lived 'in a state of complete trust, dependence and interdependence with nature'. Laurence Van der Post, writing about the extermination of the bushman says, 'He was destroyed not so much for what he did but for who he was.' Both white and black saw reflected in his apricot face the contentment of one who is always at home, who wants for nothing, who has nowhere to go and nothing to attain. The bushmen had no notion of possession, coveted nothing, lusted after nothing. He was dangerous because, by his very being, he represented that long lost corner of the European soul that no amount of 'civilisation' can ever quite make up for. 'I think', says

Van der Post, 'one of the main causes of the uncompromising ferocity with which the Bushmen had been persecuted originated precisely in the fact that he was a living image of what we had rejected and betrayed of our own aboriginal spirit. We had hoped, unconsciously perhaps, that if we killed him off in the world we would no longer be reminded of our deed of betrayal and could be at peace with ourselves.'

But it cannot be. Until the original spirit in us is given back its rightful place within, 'we will remain disastrously at war with ourselves as we had been with the bushmen in the world without' (Van der Post, 1975).

Dionysus is the god of the (ab)original indigenous spirit that experiences its effortless bliss and its oneness with the natural world. It is not for nothing that this dark god is also called 'he who wanders in the night', 'the delight of mortals' and 'the joyful one'. He is at the heart of 'walkabout', the anxiety free aimlessness of the one who has nothing to prove, whose doing comes out of being rather than out of panic, the joyousness of the one for whom, moment to moment, the universe is providing all that is essentially required. This is Christ's faith, Buddha's non-attachment, the Zen Master's 'sitting', the Brahmin's experience of Atman.

The true self is always seeking experience and expression. We may kill off the aboriginals of the world in the hope that we may hide from our shame and self-betrayal, but the Dionysian spirit that is their advocate cannot be slain, it can only be demonised. It fights an ever more covert war of attrition from its base in the unconscious, leading forays into conscious life, attacking the installations of the false self and disrupting the compliance of our bad faith. It subverts the goal-oriented intentions of compulsive doing and busyness, committing little acts of sedition that strip away the fake veneer, that sabotage the best laid plans of mice and men, compelling us into authenticity just as a streamlet is compelled to find the ocean irrespective of the dams and canals that are placed in its path.

A fine example from history is the resistance and subtle sabotage within Stalin's Gulag of Russian labour camps by the free-spirited men and women imprisoned and repressed precisely for failing to adapt themselves to the imposed regime. Despite their dire circumstances and extreme constraint they wreaked havoc on the economic infrastructure in any number of tiny but significant ways. Stalin repressed the true self of the people, killed 40 million of them, imprisoned twice that number for the most measly acts of self-determination, but his system collapsed despite the barbed wire and the thought police.

The reality of the true self impresses itself on the person despite their compliance and self-betrayal in the form of suffering. This is why our suffering is so indispensable and why 'getting rid' of symptoms is fatal to the emergence of selfhood. Suffering is the last cry of the true self before it fades from view, taking our aliveness and sense of self with it.

My individuality [says Fritz Zorn] consists of the pain I feel. I could resign myself and make peace with the idea that I just am the way my parents made me. But then I would be betraying that little part of myself I have called 'my true self'. If I resigned myself to my situation and suffered less from what I am, I might not even die of my misery. I might go on living. But then

I would have saved the part of my life I abhor most at the cost of the only part that still remains unpoisoned. Then my defeat would be even more ignominious than before, because I would become a traitor to myself. The fact that I have not done this remains, despite all else, a small victory I can claim within this otherwise vast and crushing defeat.

Without access to the authentic suffering that is the true self's subjugation and cry for help, it must resort to underhand means in order to get the compliant personality to sit up and take notice. The Dionysian spirit visits its transforming destructiveness on contrived and falsified ego structures, not out of the primitive and jealous vindictiveness of Gordius or Cybele, but does this dispassionately in order to return the person to a more real sense of themselves.

Peter consistently destroys his relationships despite his intentions. He smothers his partners, makes hugely unrealistic demands upon them, experiences a few weeks of high intensity and is then dashed on the rocks of rejection and unrequited love. Peter despairs of this tendency to become a desperate child in his love affairs. He speaks disparagingly and hatefully of himself, asking me to help him 'resolve' his problem and to become more mature.

His problem however, is not his immaturity, but his false image of being so sophisticated and debonair that excludes, with an almost tyrannical persecution, his more vulnerable and anxious aspect that is personified in his experience and his imagination as a desperate child hungry for love. The more he pushes this 'incompatible' part of him into the background the more it is compelled to sabotage his life in order to get noticed. The simple being of who he is, becomes construed as an inner enemy to be run down and persecuted at every opportunity. But this enemy will not sit still. It fights back, destroying his every effort to become other than himself, upsetting all his attempts at counterfeiting his soul and exposing his suave pretence for what it is, an exercise in unreality.

Little by little, Peter faces the terror of simply being what he is that has always implied rejection and abandonment and experiences, like Midas, the 'destructiveness' of the dark god that pulls apart the false self with wild abandon, rubbing his nose in his inauthenticity, self-hatred and bad faith. This collapse can well feel like disintegration and madness. 'What is called psychosis is sometimes simply the sudden removal of the veil of the false self, which had been serving to maintain an outer behavioural normality that may, long ago, have failed to be any reflection of the state of affairs in the secret self' (Laing, 1960). Such 'going mad' is a return to sanity, a sanity however, that is so foreign, so alien to the compliant and adapted self, that it looks like insanity itself. Both Peter and Midas have become so compliantly identified with the intrusive parent, so dismissive and envious of their original natures that return to them is experienced as a great dismembering blow, a feeling of profound disorientation.

Despite our pursuit of ecstasy, the quest for oneself, the great efforts we put into becoming who we most truly are, we must, at one and the same time, frustrate our every effort. Ecstasy is taboo in our culture, regardless of the huge 'human growth' industry that exists and even flourishes. This is because the bliss that ecstasy advocates can never be achieved under the banner of the acquisitive values we subscribe to in our heart of hearts. We must conceal this knowledge from ourselves in order not to despair of the impasse we have created, and the false self must be allowed to live and breathe in order not to experience our sick society as sick, or be too horrified by its ghastly predicament. In the meantime our bliss is held up as an ideal to be striven towards but one that remains strangely beyond our reach.

We want to have our cake and eat it. We want both our bliss and the preservation of the Hyperborean status quo us we comfortably know it. We cannot call them incompatible. That would entail naming the false compliant self for what it is. It would entail the acknowledgement that, if truth be told, we prefer our illusions and our false notions to our bliss, no matter how much we uphold the latter. We actually value 'normality' over ecstasy and must do so if we are to continue with the pleasing notions and smug self-satisfactions we have spent so much time bringing up to a shine.

'I wish to emphasise', says R.D. Laing (1960), 'that our normal adjusted state is too often the abdication of ecstasy, the betrayal of our true potentials ...' Such realisations can never be common place because they involve the humble admission of one's inauthenticity, the shame of having betrayed oneself, the guilt of wasted years and vain pursuits, the horror of one's self-estrangement, the grandiosity one's puffed up pomposity. Such experiences are profoundly corrosive. For Midas, the full realisation of just how empty, destructive and puerile was his wish induces a massive and sudden descent into depression, a feeling of dismemberment and the full appreciation of how alone and void is his world.

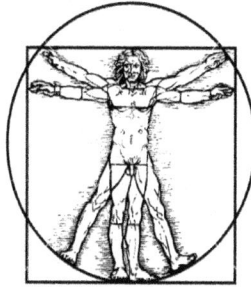

9
Chaos and Creativity

The key to victory is to throw yourself in and see what happens.
Napoleon

According to classical mythology, one of Midas' claims to fame is that he discovered black and white lead. This seems a curious and perhaps superfluous detail until we consider lead as a symbol of his saturnine depression. Moreover, the need of the self-destructive character, with his fragile ego, to have very definite opinions, necessitates seeing everything in terms of black and white. The possibility of contradiction, uncertainty, or paradox, must not test his already depleted resources too severely.

Midas bolsters his fundamental lack of selfhood by being supremely certain about things, the more certain and the more sweeping his certainties the better. This might make the Midas character feel better about himself momentarily, but it tends to evoke even more destructiveness in his relationships since such sweeping and definite perspectives are rarely open to dialogue or negotiation which is the very basis of healthy relationship. Soon his exclusive opinions render him into a club of one where his intolerance of difference makes him unable to touch others lest they contaminate his solitary but consistent hell.

Midas must seal himself off from intimacy in order to keep the part that he plays in his own suffering unconscious. His isolation increases. His suffering intensifies. He punishes himself further for the encroaching upon consciousness of these feelings of vulnerability and loneliness and in so doing further alienates himself both from his own humanity and from the humanity of others. Such an aloneness deprives him of a context in which to grapple with his issues and so his neurosis escalates and his despair increases.

Nevertheless, Midas continues to defend himself with absolute certainties and cast-iron truths in the attempt to shore up the collapsing walls of his little citadel. What would become of him without a battalion of definite opinions to defend the ramparts against all the hues of grey that threaten to throw his world into chaos and confusion? And yet, ironically enough, the desire to preserve oneself from life's chaos is exactly that which induces both chaos and self-destructiveness. 'If I want to be separate from the flux of life', says Alan Watts, 'I am wanting to be separate from life itself. Yet it is this very sense of separation that makes me feel insecure ...the desire for security and the feeling of insecurity are the same thing' (Watts, 1954).

A man once asked me, with genuine sincerity in his voice, 'but if you didn't think in terms of black and white you'd go mad, wouldn't you?' The answer is, 'Yes, perhaps', but the real question is whether or not a person's experience is authentic and an expression of the true self. The genuine despairing of Midas' psychic collapse in Dionysus' camp when he realises the extent of his self-destructiveness, the degree of his self-betrayal and the underlying circumstances that spawned it all, are surely preferable to that form of sanity which simply steers a straight course on automatic pilot through the skies of collective opinion while the true self lies gagged in the hold and the real individuality of the person held destructively hostage.

'The world', says philosopher Sören Kierkegaard, 'has generally no understanding of what is truly horrifying' (Kierkegaard, 1949). It is precisely our inability to experience despair and chaos that robs us of selfhood and compels us into destructive behaviour. When Midas stops defending himself, stops idealising his past, stops having to see things in black and white, his authentic chaos and legitimate suffering is the beginning of being returned to himself. Midas' collapse is not that of madness, but of initiation.

Such a despairing catharsis is a great step forward for Midas compared to the invisible socially adjusted despair of his former worldliness, the kind of despair in which 'a person forgets himself, dares not believe in himself, finds being himself too risky, finds it much easier to be like others ...a copy, a number' (Kierkegaard, 1949). Midas' chaos and despair is the despair of having forgotten 'his own name', the impact of realising his failure to be himself, the horror of his betrayal 'with all its attendant circumstances and ramifications' (Miller, 1990).

Midas' collapse into chaos is an appropriate response to his situation. The realisation of his destructiveness is reminiscent of another Greek king, Creon, who also brought death and destruction upon himself. He too, descends into authentic chaos:

> *I know not where I should turn*
> *Where look for help*
> *My hands have done amiss, my head is bowed*
> *With fate too heavy for me.*
>
> *(Sophocles: Antigone)*

We tend to view such collapses and chaotic conditions as being consistent with madness. Phrases like 'mad with passion', or 'crazed with grief' seem to suggest this, yet nothing could be further from the truth. We might even argue that it is actually the capacity to bear our chaos and to be present to both the horror of having colluding with it all that is the beginning of emerging out of the false and compliant self into a more genuine experience. 'It is ...the immoderation of my pain that ultimately emancipates me, despite all else, from my family and my past' (Zorn, 1982).

Such chaos and suffering is not the perpetuation of patterns designed to preserve oneself from the unknown, but a real descent into the inner world that our self-destructiveness has been designed to either ward off or fill up. Once Midas stops pushing away his despair, this void 'is soon filled with material from the unconscious that had previously censored and kept at bay. All that was secretly feared in the past, that was inflicted on one in one's early years and kept repressed in the depths of silence, is now released' (Israel, 1982).

The secret that Midas is being initiated into isn't any more or less than that which lies deep within his own soul. His descent into chaos is a descent into the arcane realities of his own unlived life which now well up into his mind's eye once he liberates himself from his vain gold-making and sees his destructiveness for what it is - a running away from himself and the reality of his aloneness.

For many years Midas has numbly endured his chaos and his despair, blocking out his authentic reality with untold acts of self-sabotage and destructiveness. Now, he faces himself. Though what he sees is 'the lonely grief-rage of powerlessness and unassuaged loss and longing' (Perera, 1980), there is a sense of being returned to himself that sustains Midas through this dark night of inner death and destruction that he has been enacting for so long.

The paradox of Midas' descent into chaos and despair is that his enacted gold-making begins to become an inner process. The making of gold that has fascinated the alchemists of all ages was never meant to be an outer operation but an inner one which depended upon the adept securing the 'prima materia', his unadulterated and authentic experience. This 'massa confusa', was both a symbol and an experience of inner chaos also named poetically enough, 'the orphan'.

The alchemists recognised that to truly become oneself necessitates an experience of chaos. It was the 'sine qua non of any regeneration of the spirit and the personality ... the basis for the preparation of the philosophical gold' (Jung, 1944). This is made possible by virtue of the fact that the 'massa confusa' contains within it the seeds of new life. This is why the alchemists got so excited by the state of mind that modern man and particularly modern psychiatry is so quick to get rid of. Hoghelande, a Dutch alchemist of the fifteenth century, wrote of chaos, 'there is nothing more wonderful in the world, for it begats itself and gives birth to itself' (from Jung, 1944). In other words we experience our own selfhood through distillations of chaos.

The alchemists equated chaos and the 'massa confusa' with the initial stage of the process of individuation, the nigredo, a despondent experience of darkness, depression and 'putrefaction', the rotting and stripping away of the false self in which there is bound to be an experience of disintegration and loss; to quote Morienus, an 'affliction of soul' (Morienus in Jung, 1944, Vol. 12, p. 273). This chaotic affliction is 'universally exemplified in the myth of the hero ... to show that only in the region of danger can one find the treasure hard to attain' (ibid., p. 335). For Midas, this treasure is his own self, but he must journey a while in chaos before he can find it.

If we look at the creation myths of different cultures we find that they all have in common an initial state of undifferentiated chaos. Out of this face of the Deep emerge the gods or the first man, and from this all of creation is made manifest. There seems to be an overriding and unavoidable message in all this that creation is contingent upon chaos. This is as true for the microcosm of the individual as it is for the macrocosm of the universe. Without initial chaos nothing ensues.

When we push our chaos away we also push away the seed of creativity that is contained within it and life becomes dry, sterile and dull. More often than not our neurosis is not so much a pocket of malevolence in the unconscious as it is the result of trying to avoid our inner chaos and the painful disorientation that accompanies it. Self-destructiveness from this point of view, is un-lived chaos and when Midas begins to experience the humbling effect of his chaos rather than acting it out, his neurosis subsides and he is returned to himself.

Chaos is the beginning of wisdom. It points unarguably to the inadequacy of our world constructs and the failure of our belief systems to really support us. When we despair in this chaos we are forced to acknowledge the limitations of the way we have things set up for ourselves. We are compelled by our discomfort to go deeply within ourselves in order to find something more sustaining. When we push our despair away, we also nip in the bud that emerging body of inner wisdom and selfhood that ever follows in its wake. Chaos and creativity, the expression of the true self, are experienced together. Any work of art is preceded by a void of blank canvas, a sculpture by a dead lump of stone, a piece of music by any number of possibilities.

In order to write this book, I have to endure not knowing, confusion, insecurity, the chaos of unnumbered pages strewn about the room and disconnected fragments lurking in questionable corners. Half-formed ideas, vague references, obscure quotes of more obscure origins, inspired thoughts hastily scribbled at night that make no sense by day but resist my waste bin with a fierce tenacity. They skitter round my desk for weeks on end, refusing to be pinned down or made accountable. Somewhere in the wings the muse responsible for all this anarchy waits patiently to see what her student will do, quite innocently planning all sorts of cruel and unusual punishments should he deign to lay aside her curse/gift in favour of an easy life.

The Gods are not in favour of our vain attempts to preserve the status quo, or of the ego's plaintive efforts to secure a little peace by turning its back on the complexity of soul. When we assume a combative stance against the opposites of Eusebes and Machimus, which are none other than the richness and variety of soul, we cannot help but incur the wrath of the muse who is bound to visit bearing a good solid neurosis.

We try to deal with chaos by identifying ourselves with portions of the psyche that do not contradict one another. We plug for congruent images of ourselves that do not demand the arduous task of living with paradox, pain or internal contradiction. When we identify with an image that does not demand too much of us, our complexities go underground and rather than being complex we are compelled to develop a complex. The soul will have it's expression.

Sooner or later we learn that the creative impulse is conceived in the womb of chaos. That chaos may be the turmoil of our unremembered past, a vortex of feeling that some stroke of fate evokes from hitherto unknown recesses of the soul or perhaps a scary step into the fullness of our potential and the fear of the dark that goes with it. The only choice we have in all this is between chaos and neurosis. They look pretty much the same until chaos subsides and like the cosmogonic myths of all time bears the creative moment.

It is difficult to put aside having to think in terms of black and white, to acknowledge that you do not know your own mind with certainty. It seems like an admission of weakness, as though you somehow lacked substance. When such lack of certitude is as a result of having the basis of one's character eroded by Gordius and Cybele this certainly does lend the personality a kind of insubstantiality, but the inner chaos under discussion is not one of having been so intruded upon that one cannot know one's own thoughts and feelings. It is rather the confusion that arises when we bravely plunge into life and allow ourselves to be beset by the complex and opposing stimuli that a rich and varied personality cannot help but entertain with ambivalence and bewilderment.

It is understandable that we should resist such a descent into disintegration, especially when the state being entered into induces 'a keen and painful sense of intellectual incompetence, a loss of will power and self-control, indecision and an incapacity and distaste for action' (Assagioli, 1965).

Should the Midas character refuse to bear the confusion and chaos that arises in the tension held between opposites, then despite his sunny appearance, the presence of Eusebes and Machimus cannot be borne and they will retreat back into 'outer space', the unconscious, where Midas' potential and possibility for growth is destructively held in suspended animation. His anxiety hides behind his arrogant black and white opinions. He manages to dress up his insecurity as a fount of authority whence he dispenses cast-iron opinions he ill suspects have as their covert purpose the task of riveting back together his underlying fragility. Such an attitude must stamp viciously on the creative possibility.

I recall a man who moved to France, bought a 16th century farmhouse and settled down in a rural village. On the surface of things he professed great love for all things French. He idealised their ways, their cooking, their countryside. Yet beneath it all he would not allow the creative chaos of really assimilating the French spirit or the disruption that his move engendered. This became most strikingly apparent when he haughtily announced that there was no point in learning French since, now that they were part of the European Union, they would have to learn to speak English! In reality he looked down on them as a way of defending against the threat that their otherness posed to his little world. He built a large English hedge around his 'corner of a foreign field' and retired behind it. The creative possibilities available to him were firmly pinched in the womb.

Needless to say our English country gentleman didn't last long in his idyll abroad. When we refuse Dionysus' offer of the opportunity for creative change we are compelled back into the familiar yet suffocating environs of yesteryear. For the want of our ambivalence, uncertainty and not knowing our lives become dry and brittle.

Our difficulty is that we have come to equate ambivalence with not caring. Something about which we are ambivalent is something to be dismissed, like the people of Eusebes and Machimus, the opposites that are dismissed into outer space. We deal with events or feelings that evoke contradictory impulses in us by demeaning them or poo-pooing them. In this way we preserve our definite opinions and with them our definite sense of self. We feign strength of purpose, appear resolved and yet something indefinable is killed off in the process; to quote Lao Tzu, 'the hard and the strong are companions of death'. Our black and whiteness tramples underfoot the creative becoming of the unfolding self.

It is for this reason that the path to selfhood is one of suffering. The definite black and whiteness of ego structures which use knowledge as a defence against being and becoming are relinquished. Not to know is to acknowledge one's smallness, the degree to which one has become lost, the extent of one's former arrogance, the arbitrariness of one's prior opinions.

We imagine that it is our conflict that constitutes our suffering. People come into therapy wanting to be relieved of their conflicts, but this is precisely the source of their suffering! They suffer, not because they are in conflict but because they refuse to live their conflict. Their task is to learn to bear their conflicts, to stop fighting life, to stop childishly wishing it were all easier. 'If you say no to it and do not accept it', says analyst Von Franz (1993), 'then, since you are not in it, it grows against you, and then it is your own inner growth which kills you'.

When we commit the sin of omission that is the refusal to jump into life with all its paradoxes and contradictions, life becomes antagonistic towards us, visits self-destructive neuroses upon us and forces us to lie on the sterile pallet we have made for ourselves. Keeping oneself safe from chaos and conflict is fatal. When we try to control fate we betray our soul's inner unfolding and must invite violence upon ourselves in the process.

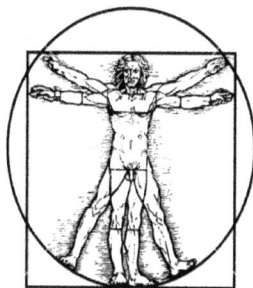

10
Suicide and Sacrifice

If you have to kill yourself, try not harm your body.
S. Johnson

Self-destructiveness is doing on the outside what needs to happen on the inside. It's a neurotic substitute for the trials of transformation that Dionysus has to offer. When Dionysus offers us a wish we must choose carefully, for we are being challenged to make a choice that champions the psyche as a whole and not just the narrow and exclusive ego structures of the personality. A wish that results in self-destruction points to some facet of the psyche that is being ignored, one that is having to break some of the planks in the soul's front door with its banging. It is not enough to see self-destructiveness just as a symptom of hidden family truths, or even as a defence mechanism against unwanted realities. We need also to ask, unlikely as it may seem, whether or not there may be some intrinsic meaning to self-destruction that does not or will not he reduced to a problem we have to solve.

Without the possibility of failure and destruction there is no risk in the heroic venture. Implicit in this is the sense that there might be meaning and purpose to be found in self-betrayal or self-destructiveness. It is not just pathological but also has something to do with the process of individuation and the finding of one's limits. As soon as we begin to have a moral attitude towards self-destructiveness we prevent ourselves from seeing clearly the nature of the issue at hand.

When Peter becomes distressed, he cuts himself with a razor blade. His arms and legs are covered with scars. After some months he comes in and shows me where he has carved the words, 'Love Hate Love' on his upper arm. He says, 'It's a signpost. I feel guilty but it's something I need to do, to make a statement. I'm pointing to something.' I ask what that might be. He doesn't know. I suggest he might be pointing to something inside him, that this outer wounding is a reminder of an inner wound that is too difficult or painful to be in touch with directly. He agrees. 'I can't see what it is, and I come over so strong; this to let the world know what a bad way I'm in. My edifice is now in ruins.' For the first time in weeks he looks touched by his predicament as he's able to share with both me and himself an experience that cannot be communicated otherwise.

Through the destructive impulse the soul is making a symbolic statement. The task of the therapist/analyst is not to persuade the client otherwise, or simply to 'resolve the pathology', but to work with the client in attempting to appreciate what the suicidal or self-mutilating impulse means to him, where it's pointing. Invariably, the desire to kill oneself, or harm oneself, is a symbolic gesture that requires the end of some long standing identification, an attachment to an idea of oneself that is itself now destructive or harmful to the rest of the psyche.

Tonight's *Star Trek* offers a wonderful example. A man has been commander of his space ship for thirty years. His ship (and his command of it) is lost in a fight. His identity is in tatters. Who is he now? Just a rescued passenger on the starship *Enterprise*. Finally, against orders, he sacrifices his life to engage an alien. Is this bravery or is it simply the fate of a man for whom life now holds no meaning? His self-destructiveness is an enactment of what needs to happen – metaphorically, the giving up of an identification with captaincy in the interests of a broader way of knowing himself We are bound to enact deeper processes and destroy ourselves to the extent that we are conditionally alive like this. For as long as our meaning and sense of self is tied or bound to one particular form of conscious expression, we will suffer and we will destroy ourselves - as though the limiting identification were not destructive enough!

Alcatraz! A prisoner passes his sentence painting. It has become his only way of staying in one piece in this terrible place. Suddenly his painting rights are taken away by the Governor. Then perhaps a week later, he chops his hand off in the woodwork shop with an axe.

We can't reduce this to the vicissitudes of negative parents. Perhaps there is a strong element of internalised rage in such behaviour, but we need to look at the specifics – he chopped off the hand that painted. Why that, of all the possibilities? What meaning is there in such a statement? Only the painter knows, and he is carted off never to be seen again, but we can guess. We can guess that the hand chopping was a symbolic piece of enactment that represented the inner need to disidentify from the painter inside him in order for him to continue to survive in the jail.

We find another tragic example of the self-destructive effects of exclusive identification with just one aspect of consciousness in Gogol's *The Overcoat*. The protagonist, Akakyevich, begins to orientate his entire life around the acquisition of a new overcoat. The ultimate theft of the coat also robs his life of meaning, so much had he invested in it, and he soon dies a miserable death. It is perhaps of no small significance that the first of the Buddha's four 'noble truths' is that attachment is the source of all suffering.

Anything with which we are unconsciously identified, controls us and compels us to find our meaning and purpose through that channel only. But fate is unkind and often dams the channel, forcing us to look elsewhere for succour. The psyche does not easily tolerate imbalance and it is bound to rebel against our becoming overly attached to just one corner of psychological life. Circumstances will inevitably conspire to thwart our efforts to remain safe.

Identifying with exclusive images of ourselves may be safe, known, secure ...but it is also limiting and an escape from life. Such images, like metaphorical gods with clay feet, must crumble for the sake and evolution of the psyche as a whole. If we do not destroy them and submit to Dionysus' instruction, some hidden hand within will begin to do the job for us.

The assumption here is that the impulse to self-destructive behaviour is not fundamentally unhealthy. When we think of self-destruction, we need to ask, 'what self is being destroyed, and to what purpose?' An inflated identification with ego-consciousness that stifles the rest of psychic life needs to be destroyed. Some incarnations of the hero secretly require the Gods' ambivalence to this end since their quest is inevitably ego-centred (my quest, my vision, my purpose) and actually needs a measure of divine ambiguity in order to regain a sense of human proportion. To realise this and to begin to act upon it may defuse the psyche's need to further impress the fact upon us with literally enacted bouts of symbolic self-destruction.

Another way of putting this is that the impulse to self-destruction has something to do with the drive for self-transcendence and transformation. On the one hand self-destructiveness 'mollifies the wrath of the Terrible Mother' (Jung, 1954) as a sacrifice appeases the Gods, but it also has the quality of renunciation, a sense of giving something up in order to regain a new form. This new form is psychological rebirth. Whatever the self-destruction, it has at its core this impulse to new life and in so far as self-destruction is a sacrifice of oneself there is implied some form of self-transcendence. This is because self-sacrifice is the giving up of an egoistic claim. The power which suppresses this egoistic claim, says Jung, 'must be the self. Hence it is the self that causes me to make the sacrifice, nay more, it compels me to make it' (Jung, 1942).

In its undistorted form self-destruction is an act of renunciation, letting something die for the sake of something more fundamental. When Midas faces what he has done, the moment when he stops protesting and surrenders to the collapse that constitutes the realisation of his former pride and egoism, he is both the destroyer and the destroyed. He rises above his habitual conception of himself, expanding both consciousness and identity, a rebirth at a developmentally more complex and integrated level of psychological organisation begins.

Self-destructive behaviour is a substitute sacrifice for the real acts of ritual transformation over which Dionysus presides. Ken Wilbur calls this 'Translation'. Instead of an old out-moded ego structure being destroyed in order to be reborn at a higher level of organisation, there is a substitute destruction of the body, or of potential, to take the place, as best possible, of a failed or incomplete transformation.

'Transformation is a type of vertical shift or mutation in consciousness structures, while translation is a simple horizontal movement within a given structure.' The purpose of translation and hence of self-destructiveness is 'to maintain the given level of the self-system, to hold it stable and constant'.

A fledgling that breaks its own wings is not going to be booted out of the nest. Self-destruction slows down the process of personal growth which in turn slows both the prospect of separation and the separation period itself, giving time to prepare for it and to manage it more effectively. Self-destructive behaviour is a way of avoiding the horror of premature separation, or the memory of it, without having to be conscious of the horror itself.

'The separate self', says Wilbur, 'will not accept transcendence, for that involves death and real sacrifice - so it substitutes token sacrifices ...bribes for the gods.' He cites the practice of chopping off fingers amongst the Crow Indians - a mystical barter system to buy more life for the self and avoid its ultimate dissolution', the dissolution of both death and its symbolic counterpart, transcendence.

To avoid the instantaneous death of transcendence, people kill themselves slowly and by degrees, dismembering their own Natures in order to preserve their own selves. The individual ... will dismember, alienate and project out of his self-system any aspect which threatens death or can be used in barter against it. (Wilbur, 1981).

Rather than experience the ego death of transcendence and psychological transformation we 'kill ourselves by degrees'. The choice is not whether we destroy ourselves or not, but whether we consciously surrender to the ego death of transformative evolution or unconsciously enact it in our efforts to preserve the status quo.

In our culture, where there is so much emphasis on 'getting it together', on integrating and developing a strong coping ego, it's inevitable that the gods exact their price for such one-sided emphasis on human rationality and personal problem solving. That price will be either the psychological self-surrender of turning away from our egocentricity in which there is also Dionysus' gift, or self-destruction, in which there is little save the reminder that we presume too much.

If we disregard Silenus, or insult Dionysus with a request that is a mere trifling, then we're headed for trouble. If we then presume to attribute their qualities to ourselves as Midas does with his arrogant desire to be the author of miraculous creations, then we will soon fail to remember our human limitations and destroy ourselves when we stray beyond the bounds of what is humanly possible. This can only have disastrous consequences. Once we have lost sight of our limitations we can only rediscover them the hard way, by overreaching ourselves.

Why then would we enter so blithely into the jaws of the unconscious? It may well be that we need to identify with the powerful archetypes of the collective in order to compensate for unbearable feelings of worthlessness and inferiority. Unable to go to our own parents for succour and solace, we go to the Great Mother or the Great Father instead, we transcend our misery by identifying with transpersonal realms. Is it perhaps just co-incidental that the flower power culture of the sixties, a mass phenomenon of collective inflation, was also the generation that, twenty years previously, lost their parents to war and evacuation?

The problem with searching for parental succour from the Gods is the role in which such a need leaves the child. The mortal offspring of the Gods are always heroes and supermen, ideals beyond mortal attainment. When a child, out of the personal need to compensate for inadequate parenting, relates to the divine as a supernatural substitute, it also brings upon itself divine expectation. The child, like Midas, is then bound to overreach itself and rediscover its mortal limitations with potentially mortal consequences. Speaking of fatherless children M.L. Von Franz says, 'Such a child feels that in reality he or she is probably a prince or a princess. Such fantasies, even when not conscious, can have an influence on the behaviour of a child and may be the basic cause of an estrangement from reality and a lack of adaptation.'(1993) When a child identifies with an ideal it must lose sight of its own humanity and evoke destructiveness on itself as a result.

I wonder sometimes whether this omnipotent identification with the hero, and the inevitable self-destructiveness that follows is what makes it possible for countless young men of every generation to march off so gaily to the killing fields of other people's wars. They have ceased to be their mother's sons and instead have become the sons of their country, mythical heroes, armies of light against forces of darkness. Having transcended their human condition to one of semidivinity they have no fear of death because in this archetypal realm death does not exist. They are forcibly reminded of their mortality in due course and even the survivors of battle cannot celebrate their escape from the jaws of death because they are too busy coming to terms with the depressing reality of their 'mere humanity', having had their illusions forcibly stripped by the dark god who will always impress upon us the errors of our inflation.

This identification with the heroic offspring of the Gods is bound to be exacerbated, by parents who, because of their own loss of faith or religious orientation, 'involuntarily identify themselves with the magic role of the Great Mother and then project the archetypal image of the hero on to their son/daughter - to the point of even preferring [their] death to the possibility that s/he might lead an ordinary human existence' (Von Franz, 1993). This antipathy to the 'merely mortal' coupled with the overreaching of the child who is unwittingly identified with the archetypal hero, creates a potent, self-destructive mix of influences.

A young man I knew, had, as a young child, a mother and a nanny who were amphetamine and opium addicts respectively. Constantly inhabiting the archetypal realms such drugs make available, they were quite literally 'cosmic mothers'. He had projected onto him the divine son as well as needing, by virtue of their human absence, to identify with archetypal contents in a precocious and compensatory manner.

Hearing about all this over the weeks made me wonder how this particular hero would overreach himself. In the spirit of the castrato he lacked the wild abandon that gets so many of his fellow heroes into trouble. It turned out, in characteristically passive fashion, that he poisoned himself with asbestos clearing out a cellar. 'I knew the asbestos was down there', he told me with a puzzled expression, 'and I knew it was toxic … I just … didn't think it would affect me.'

Despite the individual tragedies and irredeemable consequences of inflation's self-destructiveness, it may be that all this is necessary to the individuation process, at least for those who survive long enough to individuate. Being laid low by the hidden hand of Dionysus is the psyche's way of helping us regain some sense of human proportion, a more realistic appraisal of our human limitations. It divests us of illusion. In any case we can't help but become inflated when we first come in contact with that which transcends us. Like children we stumble and fall a lot between crawling and walking, of necessity becoming either identified with or running in terror from the Psyche before we can come into some kind of equitable relationship. Treading this thin line is a process of trial and error. No one gets it right first time. Midas treads either side of this line in his relationship with Dionysus. His arrogant swaggering into the dark god's camp soon becomes a cold terror of utter deflation. Both these extremes seem to be necessary before Midas can find some way of relating to Dionysus that does not inappropriately elevate or demean himself.

.I couldn't help a wry smile on a recent visit to the Freud Museum in London, to find it crammed with images of dark divinities. Jung described the psyche as a 'self-regulating system' What was being regulated in Freud's office was plain to see. For the sake of their absence in his writing, they had to people every nook and cranny of his house instead. What we need to ask ourselves in our own lives is just what it is that is being regulated when we find ourselves steeped in self-destructive behaviour and whether it could be regulated in a way that compliments the whole psyche.

The psyche has wants and needs of the personality just as people have wants and needs of each other. When needs are not satisfied, say the need for nurturing, which can be satisfied in any number of productive ways, they tend to become exclusive and destructive 'wants' - 'I want chocolate cake'. The want for chocolate cake is exclusive and because it is symbolic, the literal satisfaction does not bring one any closer to the deeper need for nurture, even if chocolate cake is available. Excessive and compulsive sexuality is another 'want'. It too is potentially symbolic - representing perhaps a deeper need for love and affection.

Neither the chocolate craving nor the perpetual sexual itch is going to go away until the deeper needs can be acknowledged. The psyche will regulate itself, and if it cannot do so by having the personality acknowledge its deeper needs with the attendant feelings of lack or loss that accompany them, then it will regulate itself in a more restricted and symbolic way - depriving the personality of the choice since it will not make one in the whole psyche's favour.

Dionysus decrees that Midas must make a penitential journey to the fount of the river Pactolus if he is to be freed from his condition. He has to become humble, but more importantly, find out who he is other than the product of his parents. He must discover his own depths. A journey to the source is a cleansing of an old way of being, the beginning of a new life based on values that spring from the ground of one's being.

The church turned fount into font but baptismal ceremony at the waters edge pre-dates written record. It signifies atonement with God, divine protection(from oneself) and enters a new life that may well have all the same old stuff going on in it but which now has a new centre. Much of life's healing comes not in the resolution of particular issues but in that life no longer revolves around them.

I once asked my analyst Chuck Shwartz, who was also a well known potter, what he did about the desire to be rich and famous. He said, 'I tip my hat to it.'

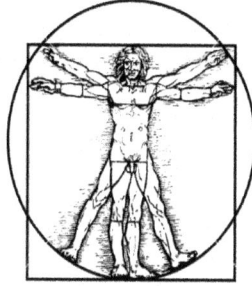

11
Self-Destruction as Symbol

If you die before you die then when you die you won't die.
Zen saying

Despite his rejuvenation in the wellsprings of soul that the source of the River Pactolus affords our hero, Midas still manages to die by his own hand. The story goes that Pan and Apollo were engaged in a contest to see who was the better player of the lyre. King Timolus, the judge of the competition, prudently awarded the prize to Apollo but Midas let it be known that he felt Pan was the better musician. Apollo rewarded his efforts by changing his ears into those of an ass. Midas was most embarrassed. He pulled his cap over his head and swore his barber, the only one ever to see his secret, to silence on pain of death.

The strain of keeping such a secret to himself was too much for the barber. In due course he dug a hole in a deserted meadow, whispered the secret into it, and then filled it back in again. All went well until some reeds grew upon the spot where the secret was buried. As they grew they murmured the secret into the wind and soon it was a secret no more. Midas was so overcome with shame that he killed himself by drinking a vessel of sacred bull's blood.

How does this happen? You might think, or at least hope, that Midas' new found atonement with the realities of his own soul and the washing away of his golden stain, would be sufficient to stem the tide of self-destructive impulses that were his family's legacy. But it is not enough simply to come to terms with the subliminal realities of our tender youth if we are to secure ourselves against the inroads of self-destructive behaviour. We must address not only the contents of the personal unconscious, but also those of the collective, for if in the process of freeing ourselves from the constraints of parental ties we become too inflated, too presumptuous, then we invite on our heads not only the retribution of parents, but also that of the Gods.

One of the reasons that the Midas syndrome has become such an epidemic today is that we have relegated the Gods from Olympus. We have lost the religious attitude (Jung, 1942). Like

Midas we only call on the Gods when we are in trouble and otherwise either dismiss them, as Midas dismisses Apollo, or we behave as though we were Gods ourselves with disastrous results.

Just as Midas drinks the sacred bull's blood, we too devour that which is not ours to have. We ravage the earth and consume both its resources and our own in ways that nature never intended. The rape of the planet is perhaps more readily witnessed, but our attitudes to our own personal natures are no less marauding. We treat our spiritual natures as commodities to be mined and harnessed to the needs of personal gratifications, as though the soul were a thing that we possessed rather than an entity which, in fact, holds us in its hand. 'The problem', says Buddhist master Chogyam Trungpa, 'is that the ego can convert anything to its own use.' We pursue a 'spiritual path' not for the sake of leaving behind our egotism, but to puff it up. 'Our vast collections of knowledge', he goes on to say, 'are just part of the ego's display, part of the grandiose quality of ego.' (1975)

We go to church in order to be seen to go to church and to be considered pious by others. We unwittingly develop acquisitive and materialistic attitudes to that very facet of life we hope might temper our grasping and image-making. We learn, not humility from our spiritual pursuits, but a kind of holier-than-thou superiority that subtly sneers at the rest of humanity and at our own all-too-human limitations and failings.

Having become acquainted with Dionysus, Midas assumes too intimate a tie with him, basks in the reflected glory of the dark god and from this position of hauteur he casts aspersions over Apollo, forgetting that Apollo and Dionysus are brothers both of whom transcend his mortal world. Apollo's punishment is fitting. The ass has ever been a lowly animal. Christ chose the ass to ride into Jerusalem as a statement of his ordinariness and humility.

We find some contemporary examples in *Pinocchio* and Shakespeare's *A Midsummer Night's Dream*. In the former, Pinocchio wakes up one day to discover that he has donkey's ears. His friend the Marmot explains, 'It is destiny. It is written in the decrees of wisdom that all boys who are lazy and who take a dislike to books, to schools and to masters, and who pass their time in amusement … must end sooner or later by becoming transformed into so many little donkeys' (Collodi, 1994).

This shaming is a punishment for puerile arrogance, for the attitude that disdains all authority and has thrown out the baby of heavenly power with the bathwater of earthly tyranny. In the process of challenging the rights of Gordius and Cybele to hold sway over his life, Midas now bows to no one. From the impotent victim he has become the cock-a-hoop bully boy and now lords it over everyone like Pinocchio - full of his own self-importance. He has mistaken contact with the Self, with becoming the Self. This leads to a huge inflation which the Gods can only experience as an intrusion and an insult.

The connection to the well spring of one's own soul … often produces a wonderful release. The preceding symptoms vanish … But, not infrequently, the personality is inadequate … The distinction between the Self and the I is blurred and the inflowing energies have the unfortunate effect of feeding … the personal ego (Assagioli, 1965).

The feeling of specialness that was the preserve of a former symbiosis with Cybele, is repeated at an archetypal level in which the poor person is bound to lose sight of his limitations and wind up self-destructively overreaching himself. Practical reality is, quite simply, not taken into consideration. I'm thinking of a young man who, beneath his depression, harboured an incredibly inflated feeling of superiority and specialness. He came to see me one day, most put out; he had been evicted from his studio. 'Oh!', said I, 'how come?' 'Well', he replied, 'I suppose it was because I didn't pay the rent!' The rent was such a piffling detail! His continued use of the place could hardly be conditional upon such a trifle! He ranted and raved about how unfair it was, really failing to see how destructive his inflation was to the day-by-day management of his affairs.

The latter example from Shakespeare, that of Bottom who is also given an ass's head, has similar connotations. Bottom 'thrusts himself into the centre of things'. He becomes the Self. He too, feels conspired against by the Gods. 'He feels he is the victim of a conspiracy', comments Brodie, 'and, most delicious of dramatic irony, it is his actual transformation into an ass that is the cause of [the others'] knavery' (Brodie, 1978). In other words, Bottom brings his fate upon himself, he destroys his standing without being aware of the part that he plays in it. It's as though he is blinded by his own inflation. After all, 'it is the characteristic of asses to be unconscious of their affliction'. Perhaps this is the thought behind the Mexican proverb, 'Only Gringos and donkeys stay out in the midday sun.' Neither party has sufficient sense of its own suffering to help or to change their situation.

Midas feels humiliated by the reminder of his ordinariness. Dionysus is, after all, his personal chum! Does that count for nothing? How difficult it is to have a personal relationship with the Gods and yet not to overreach oneself! One wonders whether the relations with God that the Christian tradition has come to embody, particularly the aspect of it that insists upon the notion of an intercessor, has as its justification and rationale - whether conscious or not - the need to place a defence between Man and God precisely to guard him against the dangers of hubris. Midas has no such luxury. He is even further disadvantaged by Cybele's legacy of specialness. He equates himself with the Gods despite, or perhaps because of Apollo's reaction to him, and drinks the sacred bull's blood - that which is the very preserve of Dionysus, the life blood of his personal totem animal.

Did Midas mean to kill himself? Was it just a last ditch attempt to remind Apollo that he had had dealings with Dionysus and was therefore someone to be reckoned with? Whatever the truth, Midas' identification with the Gods has hurried his demise.

Rather than accepting the salutary reminder of his place in the larger scheme of things that Apollo's response to him is designed to engender, Midas attempts to reaffirm his identification with Dionysus by drinking what amounts to the god's own blood, and overwhelms himself. Perhaps he takes the rebuke too much to heart and kills himself out of contrition. These possibilities sound contradictory and yet they are both part and parcel of the grandiosity/depression cycle that epitomises the self-destructive character's struggle with an ambivalent universe.

This divine ambivalence is a double bind of primordial proportions. It is one that's bound to drive Midas, who needs things to be black or white, quite around the twist. It is difficult enough for the self-destructive character to contain his own contradictions, let alone those of the Gods. He is bound to take it all personally and destroy himself out of either rageful rebellion or servile contrition for a universal problem that is not really his to shoulder.

In the Judaeo-Christian mythical tradition we also have instances of God's ambivalence and the confusion it creates for humanity. Yahweh tells Adam and Eve not to eat of the tree of knowledge but deprives them of the self-knowledge required to know right from wrong. Adam and Eve cannot exercise free will in their decision not to dally with the devil if the experience of free will can only come with the self-knowledge inherent to the apple itself. They have to eat to know that eating it is wrong. Yahweh has given them a responsibility they cannot fulfil in any meaningful way and sits back to see how they cope with their dilemma. Yahweh does this, not out of spite or vindictiveness, but because he's curious to see what will happen, just as he's curious about Job on his dung heap, Jacob sacrificing Isaac, Joseph in his pit, and ultimately Christ on the cross.

We tend to take the divinity's ambivalence towards us personally, searching our consciences for signs of sin that might account for the apparent wrath of God. We become guilty and paranoid, assuming our complicity in these visitations of a seemingly angry God, and hurry off to confess or repent or atone with self-sacrifices. Could it be that it is not the evil of humanity which accounts for God's ambivalence but that God is either having tea at the time or really doesn't give a damn one way or the other, barring a little curiosity about just what humanity actually does with its impossible situation.

If God contains all things he both has his eye on us and he does not. This ambivalence is not because he might happen to have his eye on someone else's plight and is currently busy, but because he's actually taking forty winks or laconically picking his teeth. God's omnipresence needn't mean that he is omniconcerned. Perhaps Midas even invites the Gods' wrath on himself with the inflated expectation that the psyche eternally concerns itself with the tribulations of consciousness; especially when Midas has the audacity to behave as though he were a god himself with this magical touch of his and his presumptuous taste in musical appreciation.

A grandiose client grapples with his self-importance and magical thinking over many months and finally dreams the following:

A great mountain comes to life. It is the Stone Father. This God lumbers over to an insignificant human figure and dispassionately shits on him while the latter tries in vain to protect himself with a parasol.

The Stone Father does this quite without vengefulness. There is no enmity in his action. The Stone Father is simply doing 'his job'. The (para)solar hero is brought thoroughly down to ground as a final part in the process of really humanising himself and developing a sense of proportion. It's so easy to take this as a humiliation or punishment. We do so almost out of habit, wondering what we've done to deserve this. We kick out against the Stone God and stub our toes. In the process, the warming effect of the divine turd which is gradually melting the frozen wastes of the solar hero's solitary soul is being missed.

From the perspective of the helpless human figure in the dream we might assume the God's malignity, just as Midas assumes that Apollo is against him and casts the God in the role of negative parent who has to be propitiated with acts of self-destruction which he's learnt express allegiance. Hence much of the penitential flagellation, enacted crucifixions, breast beating and mea culpas of contemporary religion. If God is unknowable, how is it that we presume that we have intimate knowledge of his slightest moods? It is precisely because God is unknowable that we find in him a convenient blank screen to experience afresh the unconscious paranoia and persecution generated by Gordius and Cybele.

An old landlady of mine who was a great bearer of crosses had, as an eternal source of aggravation, a faulty cistern in the loft. It overflowed as a result and threatened the outer brickwork of the house where it continuously ran down the wall. She would stand in the hall and mutter curses at the offending contraption. 'But it was working', she used to say, 'what have I done to deserve this? I paid good money for that cistern.' The fact that her 'good money' exchanged hands 25 years previously seemed almost incidental.

Time stands still in Hyperborea. Change and decay can only be experienced as the aggressive intrusion of an unfair fate conspiring against us like a plotting parent who we're secretly convinced is justifiably out to get us. The cistern remained unattended. The brickwork gradually rotted. The landlady shuffled about in increasing doubt about her moral rectitude, silently searching her soul for fault that God should smite her in this way sinking each day into deeper deprecation of her unknown crime, hoping perhaps that the destruction to her property was enough to atone for whatever it was that she had done.

If we are to prevent our self-destruction, sacrificial suicides and 'accidents', we must learn to bear the revelatory transformations of these deeper needs that both Apollo and Dionysus offer us - painful and humbling as they are. Some kind of meaning in suffering must be found in Dionysus' camp, some kind of discrimination between humility and humiliation in Apollo's. The Phrygian child, with his weak and undermined sense of self is being asked to make the most difficult of journeys. His helpers along the way are the very acts of self-destruction that point directly to all those unpleasant pockets of reality he must contend with, experiences that might ultimately encourage him to use his own eyes and to forge his own uncertain yet authentic path through life.

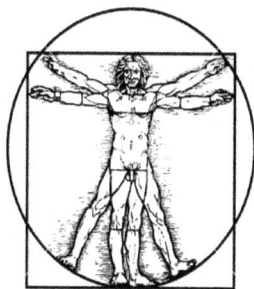

12
The Broken Wings

The problem for the hero, ... is to open his soul beyond terror to such a degree that he will be ripe to understand how the sickening and insane tragedies of this vast and ruthless cosmos are completely validated in the majesty of Being.

J. Campbell

The problem we face in trying to make sense of self-destructiveness is that we tend to do so from a partisan position. The various schools of psychology all have different takes on the phenomenon, different explanations and different solutions. None of these rich and varied positions is 'wrong'. But they are all limited by the parameters they choose to delineate their discipline. As a result they can only ever bring a partial and incomplete response to the arena of self-destructiveness, which is why it is such a difficult issue to address effectively. It requires of the therapist a breadth of vision that threatens to disrupt his or her own sense of professional identity.

If we are willing, however, to put down our allegiances in order to embrace the complexities with which we are faced, we shall all have a better appreciation of what is going on and a greater degree of comfort with what is so often strange or unintelligible.

To close, I'd like to bring all the different perspectives so far discussed to bear upon a single case history, that of the famous author and mystic, Kahlil Gibran. Or shall I say that of the relationship between Gibran and his beloved Selma, a romance that ended in family deaths and suicide. Gibran recounts the unfolding of this catalogue of self-destruction in an autobiographical account entitled *The Broken Wings*, a tragic tale of almost Grecian proportions.

The plot is simple enough. Young Gibran falls in love with Selma, daughter of a rich merchant. She, however, is promised to another, the nephew of the local bishop. Despite the father's and daughter's preference for Gibran, there seems to be no way out. The marriage takes place. Selma's father dies of a broken heart, followed soon after by his daughter, leaving Gibran bereft and grieving. All very well and thoroughly tragic, but why was it all so inevitable? Why did the rich father not refuse the bishop? He knew how unhappy the arrangement would make everyone. Why? Because if he did 'he would not remain in good standing'. In other words he sacrificed his life and his daughter's for his position in society. Attachment to and identification with his role killed him as surely as if he had slit his own throat.

This is not simply a question of honour on the father's part. Rather, it is inconceivable to him that he should have a different position in society than the one he knows. His values, his very being, are wrapped up in a relation to authority that smacks of the same kind of family scenario as that of Midas. If I dare to make myself happy, or fulfil the desires of those I love, I will be abandoned or destroyed. Not to be in good standing is a euphemism for being ostracised from that body of law whose protection is experienced as life itself. Meantime both Selma and the young Kahlil accept this state of affairs. How come? Why not run away? Presumably the same subservience to authority and negative societal injunctions is working in them, but there is more - they are afraid of freedom. 'Mention not peace', says Selma, 'its shadow frightens me.' This is rationalised by references to 'fate' and 'destiny', the great deniers of responsibility.

For those of a more analytical bent, it emerges that part of the reason that Selma's father dies after she is sent to live with her new husband is that she has been 'his only consolation' since his wife died. This is because Selma is 'the image of her mother in every deed and word'. He relates to his daughter as though she were his wife, and gives her the power to afford his life with meaning. But she cannot fulfil this ideal, and he,contingent on this, dies. Selma has failed to fit the ideal of her mother's empty shoes. Her consolation has been insufficient. Rather than rebel against the unreasonable expectation she vainly attempts to fulfil it. She tries and fails. Like Midas caught between the wildly divergent demands of his parents, Selma is trapped between either doing as she's told and abandoning her father to his broken-hearted death, or refusing and have him die from social shame. Whatever she does she has killed him.

It emerges that Selma's mother died when Selma was three. Considering the omnipotent feelings at this stage of development it would be reasonable to suppose that the infant considers herself party to her mother's death as well. Children of this age have to believe they magically cause what is going on about them. The impotence of simply being on the receiving end of an ambivalent fate is far too anxiety-provoking to entertain.

Selma is riddled with neurotic guilt, let alone the damage of incomplete or forced and premature separation from her mother. No wonder she has 'sorrowful eyes'. And what of the rage at being deprived of Mother, of having Father relate to her as though she were other than herself, and then failing to protect her from a life of slavery to a man she knows wants her only for her money? But no, Papa is wonderful, idealised, we'll put it all down to destiny. But that destructive rage has to go somewhere and since she 'chokes her voice', we can assume it stays inside and turns against her. Bearing in mind her 'guilt', this marriage is, after all, an appropriate punishment and a legitimate object for her own split-off anger that may not be otherwise expressed.

The young Gibran begins to get a sense of what is going on. He says to Selma in one of their secret meetings, 'He who extinguishes his spirit's fire with his own hands is an infidel in the eyes of Heaven, for Heaven set the fire that burns in our spirits.' He implores her to run away with him. But Selma says she 'is not worthy of love and peace'. Yet concealed in her depression and low esteem is an inflation that reaches Qlympian proportions, equating her choice for suffering with that of Christ. I wonder whether washing herself with 'blood and tears' and drinking 'gall and vinegar' is really sufficient to maintain such an exalted state, though it must surely atone her for her sins. Of course, Selma can't maintain this 'contentment' with archetypal suffering for long and dies shortly after bidding Gibran a final goodbye.

Perhaps Selma has a death wish, who knows. What would seem to be more in evidence is her self-destructiveness as a defence against the fear of death. After deciding not to see Gibran again for the sake of his 'honour', she says, 'Now I shall return happily to my dark cave where horrible ghosts reside.' It would seem that her self-denial of everything that is precious to her serves to inoculate her against the dreadful experience of the 'dark cave', a trade-off made perhaps more horrible by the Gods themselves for daring in her hubris to equate Gibran with Heaven, and for making of their mortal love a divine union.

Selma's difficulty is that she lives in a relatively symbiotic state with a father who has become both Father and Mother since her mother's death. The prospect of marriage is a death blow to this father/daughter merger. Selma is forced to realise that her father exists independently of her but she cannot acknowledge the feelings of rage against him that this evokes, nor the feelings of rejection that separation entails. The precious relationship has already been dealt a crucial blow. She cannot compound the situation. She can, however, seek a fresh merger with Gibran and turn her hate onto the Bishop and his nephew. Her destructiveness, however, and her envy of father's autonomy have nowhere to go, so she attacks herself. She attacks her own autonomy and emerging self, paying dearly for it with a freshly constellated paranoid fantasy. 'I am feeling that the house I live in and the path I walk on are all eyes watching me and fingers pointing at me and ears listening to the whisper of my thoughts.'

Selma's paradoxical association between being her father's consolation and being entitled to life, not to mention the unconscious guilt of killing her mother and the sense of debt and responsibility this gives rise to, invites her to destroy herself in order to preserve herself, throwing in for good measure the fresh opportunity to consolidate the idealisation of her father by turning the bishop into bad parent. Few children, if any, can resist this seductive role of heroically saving the parent despite the cost to themselves. It means living with anxiety, paranoid fantasies, the perpetual intangible expectation of doom - the constellation of which is almost a welcome release.

All this evokes a rage against becoming oneself. The rage and destructiveness of such an enactment are a reaction against the anxiety of becoming oneself with all its imagined consequences, and an attempt to retain the identification with the parent that at least promises a familiar if prescribed existence.

We can understand Selma's rigid adherence to social norms and the pervading sense of guilt in her relationship to Gibran as aspects of Midas' concern that he is an unworthy son. For Selma this constitutes the fear of being found out by the Bishop and the guilty supposition that she is responsible for her parents' deaths. This is accompanied by internal demands that she submit to the cultural rules of both family and society. She dutifully suppresses her hate and turns it in on herself. She is 'unworthy' of Gibran, 'fated' to be with a man she cannot love. Presumably fate can see her as she 'really' is, as so many of our clients fear to be seen as they 'really' are for fear that we will see them as they see themselves.

Despite the fact that Selma is able to split off the negative father onto the Bishop in order to preserve the ideal so threatened by the impending separation, the Bishop cannot carry it all. That would entail her explicitly marrying into a totally unacceptable situation. She has to swallow some of it herself, with the inevitable consequence that this deviates her from her intended path and consolidates her 'fate'. This heroic 'self-sacrifice', however, has a pernicious aspect since the motive is unconscious - the preservation of the ideal - and so the motif of self-sacrifice that is ever a detail of the heroic venture degenerates into self-destructiveness.

For all Selma's evocation of 'fate' and 'destiny', she is clinging to the known and assiduously avoiding the direction in which both fate and destiny seem to be ushering her. Her heroic 'bravery' is in fact a denial of personal responsibility and keeps at bay the danger of becoming too conscious of the ambivalence inherent in her relationship. She preserves a naive and romantic vision of Gibran, without having to take up her own direction. She wants to have her cake and eat it. Rather than accept the doubt and insecurity inherent in forging her own path through life, Selma submerges herself in the patriarchal power that seeks to dictate the very course of life, and by doing so she side-steps her misery, impotence and frustrated rage.

She seals herself off from intimacy or makes it into something else so that she can keep the part that she plays in her own suffering unconscious. But her isolation increases. Her suffering intensifies. She punishes herself further for the encroachment of these feelings of vulnerability and loneliness and in so doing further alienates herself from both her own humanity and the humanity of others. Such an aloneness deprives her of a context in which to have sufficient space for grappling with her issues, and so her neurosis escalates and her despair increases.

She doubts Kahlil's capacity to support her, seeing their shared grief as depleting their togetherness rather than serving as a common ground from which to draw strength. 'How can he console me?' she asks. 'I have dimmed his eyes with my tears till he can see nothing but darkness. [He] shares my sorrow and helps me shed tears which increase my bitterness and burn my heart.' Kahlil has unwittingly become Selma's persecutor. She blames him but hangs onto him. This is quite usual in the denial of responsibility since what the person wants is not so much good health but a sense of identity that even suffering can provide.

Kahlil actively, if unconsciously, supports and colludes with her suffering. This, on the one hand, is a neurotic attempt to avoid the suffering, but it is also an attempt to preserve a sense of identity in the face of the chaos and collapses she anticipates or expects from facing the truth about herself. If the person has become identified with her suffering, despite the pain involved, to give it up is also to give up identification which requires a dismantling of the status quo and so raises the fear of disintegration, madness and even death.

Selma's physical death is prefigured by a slow, emotional death. She becomes a 'scared phantom' and a 'trembling shadow' as she increasingly identifies with the archetypal realms which are fast becoming the only route out of her situation. Having had to carry her father's fantasy image of women all her life she is no stranger to such things. 'Selma sees everything through the eyes of the spirit', he says.

Her relation to Gibran is certainly thick with archetypal nuances which must impact on the relationship between them as personalities. Gibran realises this at their first meeting. 'Was I intoxicated with the wine of youth which made me fancy that which never existed?' he asks himself in a moment of reflection. Certainly the feeling towards her, 'like a spirit hovering over the waters at the creation of the world', might have warned him that something was blinding 'his natural eyes', that he was beginning to equate himself with God, and Selma with the face of the deep.

Selma is no better. 'Look at me', she says to Gibran, 'and I will show you the holy torch which heaven has lighted in the ashes of my heart ... [a] love which is born in the firmament's lap ...content with [nothing] but eternity and immortality.' Her inflationary identification with Christ is quite transparent, 'I have worn the wreath of thorns ...I have drunk vinegar and gall ... Ironically enough their self-destructiveness is, at one and the same time, a symbolic desire to atone with the divine and yet, paradoxically, the action of the god upon them for their inevitable arrogance and ambiguity.

When such a person discovers her 'merely mortal' capacities, the deprecation that follows is a fresh round of self-recrimination and abuse. 'All these thoughts which illuminate a woman's heart', says Selma, 'and make her rebel against old customs and live in the shadow of freedom and justice, made me believe that I am weak and that our love is feeble and limited ...I cried like a king whose kingdom and treasures have been usurped.'

Our task in life is to realise that we are always becoming. We are thereby eternally incomplete. We must inevitably fail, live in bad faith and have the kingdom we so keenly desire denied us. Our task is to learn to live with this without descending into a self-destructive orgy of despair like two-year-olds who smash their Christmas presents because they are not quite what they wanted.

Life can only have meaning if we allow ourselves to stay connected to possibility, the possibility of becoming; but this means opening oneself to disappointment, failure and an encounter with one's own faint-heartedness. When integrity collides with self-preservation it is like the unstoppable smashing into the unmoveable. What will happen? Which way will you jump? Either way it is a death of sorts. Self-destruction will both buy time and serve as a workable solution to the dilemma. But it is a very expensive insurance policy. Once it has drawn our attention to inner conflicts that have no other avenue for their expression, we need to find routes of resolution that are not so costly, dare to live and become even if we can no longer know who it is that dares to do so.

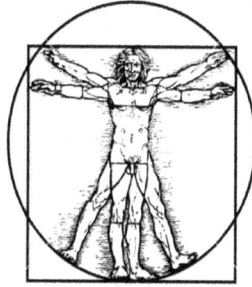

Bibliography

Assagioli, R., *Psychosynthesis* (Harper Collins, 1965)

Bion, W., *Experiences in Groups* (Tavistock, 1961)
Bronowski,_J., *William Blake* (Penguin, 1958)

Campbell. J., *The Hero with a Thousand Faces* (Paladin, 1988)
Campbell, J., *The Masks of God*, V01. 1 (Viking, 1954)
Carroll, L., *Alice in Wonderland* (Macmillan, 1865)
Collodi, C., *Pinocchio* (Bloomsbury Books, 1994)

Dabrowski, S., *Positive Disintegration* (Churchill, 1964)
Dante, A., *The Inferno* (Penguin, 1949)
Dostoevsky, F., *The House of the Dead* (Penguin, 1985)
Durkheim, E., *Suicide* (Routledge & Kegan Paul, 1951)

Eliot, T.S., *The Four Quartets* (Faber, 1944)

Ferrucci, P., *Self as Friend, Self as Fiend* (Lecture to Psychosynthesis Conference, Davos, Switzerland, 1991)
Freud, S., *On Metapsychology* (Penguin, 1955)
Fromm, E., *Fear of Freedom* (Routledge, 1942)

Gibran, K., *A Second Treasury of Kahlil Gibran* (Mandarin, 1992)
Greenberg & Mitchell, *Object Relations in Psychoanalytic Theory* (Tavistock, 1983)
Gogol, N., *The Overcoat* (Merlin Press, 1956)
Grof, S., *Realms of the Human Unconscious* (Souvenir, 1986)
Guntrip, *Schizoid Phenomena: Object Relations and the Self* (Tavistock, 1968)
Hesse, H., *The Prodigy* (Penguin, 1957)
Hillman, J., *Suicide and the Soul* (Shambhala, 1980)
Horney, K., *Neurosis and Human Growth* (Norton, 1970)
Israel, M., *The Pain that Heals* (Crossroad, 1982)

Jacoby, M., *Longing for Paradise* (Sigo Press, 1985)

Johnson, S., *Humanizing the Narcissistic Style* (Norton, 1987)
Jung, C., *Psychology and Alchemy* (Routledge and Kegan Paul, 1944)
Jung, C., *The Archtypes and the Collective Unconscious* (Routledge & Kegan Paul, 1954)
Jung, C., *Mysterium Coniunctionis* (Routledge & Kegan Paul, 1955)
Jung, C., *Psychology and Religion* (Routledge & Kegan Paul, 1942)
Jung, C., *Symbols of Transformation* (Routledge & Kcgan Paul, 1929)

Klein, M., *The Selected Melanie Klein* (Penguin, 1986)
Kierkegaard, S., *The Sickness into Death* (Penguin, 1949)
King. S. *Cape Fear* (Penguin 1987)

Laing, R.D., *The Divided Self* (Tavistock, 1960)

Miller, A., *Banished Knowledge* (Virago, 1990)

Perkins, J., *The Forbidden Self* (Shambhala, 1992)
Perls, F., et al *Gestalt Therapy* (Souvenir Press, 1972)
Perera, S., *Descent to the Goddess* (Inner City Books, 1980)
Pitt-Aikins, T. & Ellis, A., *Loss of the Good Authority* (Penguin, 1989)
Pratchett, T., *Moving Pictures* (Transworld, 1990)

Rudd, E., *Dragons* (W.H. Allen, 1986)

Sophocles, *Antigone* (Penguin, 1947)
Stettbacher,J., *Making Sense of Suffering* (Dutton, 1991)
Suttie, I., *The Origins of Love and Hate* (Routledge & Kegan Paul, 1935)
Szasz, T., *Ideology and Insanity* (Penguin, 1970)

Tennyson, A., *The Lotus Eaters* (Oxford University Press, 1907)
Trungpa, C., *Cutting through Spiritual Materialism* (Shambhala, 1975)
Tzu, L., *The Tao Te Ching* (Arkana, 1985)

Van der Post, L., *A Mantis Carol* (Penguin, 1975)
Von Franz, M., *Psychotherapy* (Shambhala, 1993)

Watts, A., *The Wisdom of Insecurity* (Rider, 1954)
Wickes, F., *The Inner World of Childhood* (Sigo, 1955)
Wilbur, K., *Up from Eden* (Routledge, 1981)
Winnicott, D., *Home is where we start from* (Penguin, 1986)
Woods & Woods, *Transactional Analysis San Francisco Journal* (International TA
                                                                    Association, 1982)

Yalom, I., *Existential Psychotherapy* (Basic Books, 1980)

Zorn, F., *Mars* (Pan, 1982)

THE WORLD'S WEIRDEST PUBLISHING COMPANY

ANIMALS & MEN
ISSUES 16-20
THE JOURNAL OF THE CENTRE FOR FORTEAN ZOOLOGY
NEW HORIZONS
Edited by Jon Downes

BIG CATS LOOSE IN BRITAIN

PREDATOR DEATHMATCH
NICK MOLLOY
WITH ILLUSTRATIONS BY ANTHONY WALLIS

...TER!
...ZOO...M PHENOMENA
Edited by
Jonathan Downes and Richard Freeman
FOREWORD BY Dr. KARL SHUKER

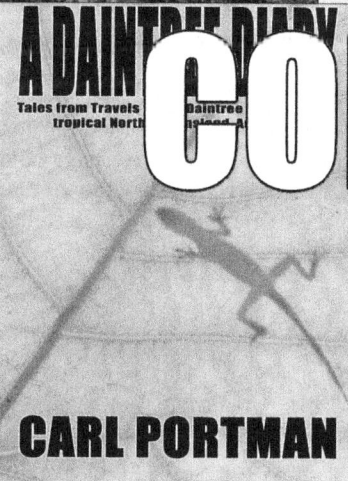

A DAINTREE DIARY
Tales from Travels... Daintree
tropical North...
CARL PORTMAN

THE COLLECTED POEMS
Dr Karl P. N. Shuker

STRANGELYSTRANGE
...ly normal
an anthology of writings by
ANDY ROBERTS

HOW TO START A PUBLISHING EMPIRE

Unlike most mainstream publishers, we have a non-commercial remit, and our mission statement claims that "we publish books because they deserve to be published, not because we think that we can make money out of them". Our motto is the Latin Tag *Pro bona causa facimus* (we do it for good reason), a slogan taken from a children's book *The Case of the Silver Egg* by the late Desmond Skirrow.

WIKIPEDIA: "The first book published was in 1988. *Take this Brother may it Serve you Well* was a guide to Beatles bootlegs by Jonathan Downes. It sold quite well, but was hampered by very poor production values, being photocopied, and held together by a plastic clip binder. In 1988 A5 clip binders were hard to get hold of, so the publishers took A4 binders and cut them in half with a hacksaw. It now reaches surprisingly high prices second hand.

The production quality improved slightly over the years, and after 1999 all the books produced were ringbound with laminated colour covers. In 2004, however, they signed an agreement with Lightning Source, and all books are now produced perfect bound, with full colour covers."

Until 2010 all our books, the majority of which are/were on the subject of mystery animals and allied disciplines, were published by `CFZ Press`, the publishing arm of the Centre for Fortean Zoology (CFZ), and we urged our readers and followers to draw a discreet veil over the books that we published that were completely off topic to the CFZ.

However, in 2010 we decided that enough was enough and launched a second imprint, `Fortean Words` which aims to cover a wide range of non animal-related esoteric subjects. Other imprints will be launched as and when we feel like it, however the basic ethos of the company remains the same: Our job is to publish books and magazines that we feel are worth publishing, whether or not they are going to sell. Money is, after all - as my dear old Mama once told me - a rather vulgar subject, and she would be rolling in her grave if she thought that her eldest son was somehow in `trade`.

Luckily, so far our tastes have turned out not to be that rarified after all, and we have sold far more books than anyone ever thought that we would, so there is a moral in there somewhere…

Jon Downes,
Woolsery, North Devon
July 2010

CFZ PRESS

Other Books in Print

Weird Waters – The Mystery Animals of Scandinavia: Lake and Sea Monsters by Lars Thomas
The Inhumanoids by Barton Nunnelly
Monstrum! A Wizard's Tale by Tony "Doc" Shiels
CFZ Yearbook 2011 edited by Jonathan Downes
Karl Shuker's Alien Zoo by Shuker, Dr Karl P.N
Tetrapod Zoology Book One by Naish, Dr Darren
The Mystery Animals of Ireland by Gary Cunningham and Ronan Coghlan
Monsters of Texas by Gerhard, Ken
The Great Yokai Encyclopaedia by Freeman, Richard
NEW HORIZONS: Animals & Men issues 16-20 Collected Editions Vol. 4
by Downes, Jonathan
A Daintree Diary -
Tales from Travels to the Daintree Rainforest in tropical north Queensland, Australia
by Portman, Carl
Strangely Strange but Oddly Normal by Roberts, Andy
Centre for Fortean Zoology Yearbook 2010 by Downes, Jonathan
Predator Deathmatch by Molloy, Nick
Star Steeds and other Dreams by Shuker, Karl
CHINA: A Yellow Peril? by Muirhead, Richard
Mystery Animals of the British Isles: The Western Isles by Vaudrey, Glen
Giant Snakes - Unravelling the coils of mystery by Newton, Michael
Mystery Animals of the British Isles: Kent by Arnold, Neil
Centre for Fortean Zoology Yearbook 2009 by Downes, Jonathan
CFZ EXPEDITION REPORT: Russia 2008 by Richard Freeman *et al*, Shuker, Karl (fwd)
Dinosaurs and other Prehistoric Animals on Stamps - A Worldwide catalogue
by Shuker, Karl P. N
Dr Shuker's Casebook by Shuker, Karl P.N
The Island of Paradise - chupacabra UFO crash retrievals,
and accelerated evolution on the island of Puerto Rico by Downes, Jonathan
The Mystery Animals of the British Isles: Northumberland and Tyneside by Hallowell, Michael J
Centre for Fortean Zoology Yearbook 1997 by Downes, Jonathan (Ed)
Centre for Fortean Zoology Yearbook 2002 by Downes, Jonathan (Ed)
Centre for Fortean Zoology Yearbook 2000/1 by Downes, Jonathan (Ed)

Centre for Fortean Zoology Yearbook 1998 by Downes, Jonathan (Ed)
Centre for Fortean Zoology Yearbook 2003 by Downes, Jonathan (Ed)
In the wake of Bernard Heuvelmans by Woodley, Michael A
CFZ EXPEDITION REPORT: Guyana 2007 by Richard Freeman *et al*, Shuker, Karl (fwd)
Centre for Fortean Zoology Yearbook 1999 by Downes, Jonathan (Ed)
Big Cats in Britain Yearbook 2008 by Fraser, Mark (Ed)
Centre for Fortean Zoology Yearbook 1996 by Downes, Jonathan (Ed)
THE CALL OF THE WILD - Animals & Men issues 11-15
Collected Editions Vol. 3 by Downes, Jonathan (ed)
Ethna's Journal by Downes, C N
Centre for Fortean Zoology Yearbook 2008 by Downes, J (Ed)
DARK DORSET -Calendar Custome by Newland, Robert J
Extraordinary Animals Revisited by Shuker, Karl
MAN-MONKEY - In Search of the British Bigfoot by Redfern, Nick
Dark Dorset Tales of Mystery, Wonder and Terror by Newland, Robert J and Mark North
Big Cats Loose in Britain by Matthews, Marcus
MONSTER! - The A-Z of Zooform Phenomena by Arnold, Neil
The Centre for Fortean Zoology 2004 Yearbook by Downes, Jonathan (Ed)
The Centre for Fortean Zoology 2007 Yearbook by Downes, Jonathan (Ed)
CAT FLAPS! Northern Mystery Cats by Roberts, Andy
Big Cats in Britain Yearbook 2007 by Fraser, Mark (Ed)
BIG BIRD! - Modern sightings of Flying Monsters by Gerhard, Ken
THE NUMBER OF THE BEAST - Animals & Men issues 6-10
Collected Editions Vol. 1 by Downes, Jonathan (Ed)
IN THE BEGINNING - Animals & Men issues 1-5 Collected Editions Vol. 1 by Downes, Jonathan
STRENGTH THROUGH KOI - They saved Hitler's Koi and other stories
by Downes, Jonathan
The Smaller Mystery Carnivores of the Westcountry by Downes, Jonathan
CFZ EXPEDITION REPORT: Gambia 2006 by Richard Freeman *et al*, Shuker, Karl (fwd)
The Owlman and Others by Jonathan Downes
The Blackdown Mystery by Downes, Jonathan
Big Cats in Britain Yearbook 2006 by Fraser, Mark (Ed)
Fragrant Harbours - Distant Rivers by Downes, John T
Only Fools and Goatsuckers by Downes, Jonathan
Monster of the Mere by Jonathan Downes
Dragons:More than a Myth by Freeman, Richard Alan
Granfer's Bible Stories by Downes, John Tweddell
Monster Hunter by Downes, Jonathan

Fortean Words

The Centre for Fortean Zoology has for several years led the field in Fortean publishing. CFZ Press is the only publishing company specialising in books on monsters and mystery animals. CFZ Press has published more books on this subject than any other company in history and has attracted such well known authors as Andy Roberts, Nick Redfern, Michael Newton, Dr Karl Shuker, Neil Arnold, Dr Darren Naish, Jon Downes, Ken Gerhard and Richard Freeman.

Now CFZ Press are launching a new imprint. Fortean Words is a new line of books dealing with Fortean subjects other than cryptozoology, which is - after all - the subject the CFZ are best known for. Fortean Words is being launched with a spectacular multi-volume series called *Haunted Skies* which covers British UFO sightings between 1940 and 2010. Former policeman John Hanson and his long-suffering partner Dawn Holloway have compiled a peerless library of sighting reports, many that have not been made public before.

Other books include a look at the Berwyn Mountains UFO case by renowned Fortean Andy Roberts and a series of forthcoming books by transatlantic researcher Nick Redfern. CFZ Press are dedicated to maintaining the fine quality of their works with Fortean Words. New authors tackling new subjects will always be encouraged, and we hope that our books will continue to be as ground-breaking and popular as ever.

Haunted Skies Volume One 1940-1959 by John Hanson and Dawn Holloway
Haunted Skies Volume Two 1960-1965 by John Hanson and Dawn Holloway
Space Girl Dead on Spaghetti Junction - an anthology by Nick Redfern
I Fort the Lore - an anthology by Paul Screeton
UFO Down - the Berwyn Mountains UFO Crash by Andy Roberts

Lightning Source UK Ltd.
Milton Keynes UK
UKOW05f1825230117
292668UK00005B/369/P